Overcome ...ur Fear
of Homeschooling
with Insider Information

SANDRA K. COOK

M.S. Instructional Design

ISBN: 1490921222
ISBN-13: 978-1490921228

DEDICATION

This book is dedicated to three faithful homeschooling
moms God put in my path:

Jill Breneman,
who first convinced me I was capable of homeschooling;

Gail Donaldson,
whose research diligence and out-of-the-box thinking
enabled me to find unique learning solutions;

and

Sylvia Vance,
a great friend and veteran homeschooling mom who
provided me great guidance and endless encouragement.

CONTENTS

	Acknowledgments	i
	Introduction	iii
1	Educational Benefits	1
2	Patience is a Virtue	19
3	The "S" Word - Socialization	33
4	Long-Term Planning	51
5	Lifestyle Transformation	77
6	Economic Survival	103
7	Conclusion	119
	References	121
	About the Author	123

ACKNOWLEDGMENTS

First, I would like to acknowledge God's Holy Spirit, who has whispered in my ear "write the book" for the past several years. His constant reminder that I have encouragement to share with others has brought this book to you.

I would like to acknowledge my dear husband, who worked tirelessly to support our family through our homeschooling years and for his encouragement during periods when I was uncertain about my homeschooling abilities.

I would also like to acknowledge my sons for the gift of learning I received while homeschooling them. I learned more from raising my boys and through our homeschooling experiences than I ever anticipated when my guys were born. They have made me a richer, more knowledgeable person.

I would also like to acknowledge my many homeschooling friends who encouraged me to write this book and who continue to support my efforts to help new homeschoolers. So many of my friends have been an encouragement to me throughout our homeschooling.

Thank you, everyone!

SANDRA K. COOK

INTRODUCTION

I never intended to homeschool my children. It was never my dream to do so as it is with some moms. No, I packed my little kindergartners' lunch boxes, hugged them, kissed them, and put them on the bus for their first day of school.

When we put our older son on the bus for his first day of kindergarten, he was exuberant, knowledgeable, and talkative. Five years later, my formerly bubbly son was becoming more depressed and sullen with each passing day, and I was seeing no meaningful education progress. By the end of fourth grade, my son's self-esteem was lower than an ant's belly: He wouldn't talk to people, and he believed he couldn't learn.

Because he had severe dyslexia, one administrator at our school told us our older son would "probably never read well." When I said I thought my son was actually gifted and he wanted to go to college, the administrator literally laughed out loud and barked, "YOU need to lower your expectations. He is NOT college material!" She shook her head at me as if I was stupid for thinking my child had any future at all.

My younger son likewise went off to public school as a creative, highly intelligent, exuberant, non-stop tornado of energy. You can probably guess how well that went! While the other second graders were learning addition and subtraction facts, my son had moved past multiplication and wanted to learn long division. At the parent-teacher conference, the teacher told us, "We can't teach him long division or he'll be even more bored next year!"

Let me tell you, a school is going to have difficulty when they have a bright child with boundless energy who is bored, sitting in a desk, waiting for everyone else to finish their work. It became clear the synergy of my son's intelligence level coupled with his boundless energy and boredom in the classroom was not going to go well for him. He began getting into trouble for his self-entertainment and clowning around, but it was clear to me that the problem was not with my son: He didn't fit into a stifling, traditional, slow-paced (for him) classroom.

Clearly, public school was not helping either of my boys. My older son's spirit was being crushed by the daily message that he was worthless because he couldn't read. My younger son was developing a reputation as a class clown. Neither boy was learning what he needed to learn in public school. We knew we had to make a change. We couldn't afford private school, so we started considering alternatives, one of which was homeschooling.

I came to the task of homeschooling kicking, crying, and fretting all the way. I had no clue how to homeschool, no clue what I was in for, and particularly no clue about how homeschooling would transform our lives. Given that we had not planned on homeschooling, I was ill-prepared to begin and felt like I was finding my way with blinders on. To put it simply: I was TERRIFIED.

I was terrified my boys would not make good educational progress.

I was terrified I might ruin their lives if I didn't school them right.

I was terrified I would not be patient enough to school them. (I wondered if we would scream at each other all the time and end up hating each other.)

I was terrified my kids would be isolated from others.

I was terrified to lose my career, my income, and my

dreams. I was a computer programmer by trade—I had no teaching background.

I was terrified of trying to make it on a single income.

I was a far cry from the confident, "I'm going to homeschool my kids," moms who knew they wanted to homeschool their children before the children were even born.

If you are a similar, reluctant mom who is considering homeschooling . . . this book is for YOU!

Looking back, my only regret is that we didn't start homeschooling SOONER. Traveling the homeschooling road is a great journey.

Let's get started!

SANDRA K. COOK

1 EDUCATIONAL BENEFITS

Schooling your child at home can bring many unexpected educational benefits. Homeschooling allows you to progress at your child's individual pace of learning, it provides learning efficiency, and it allows you to tailor your instruction to meet your child's individual needs.

Learning at Your Child's Pace

One of the great benefits of homeschooling is your child's ability to learn at his or her own pace. Whether your child masters concepts slowly or quickly, you are not constrained to a school's artificial calendar of progress.

If your child learns quickly, you can move forward as rapidly as your child is able, which allows you to cover the early learning skills of reading, hand writing, and mathematical computation in a short period of time. You can then move on to more sophisticated conceptual learning. Your child will not be held back by the overall average learning speed of a classroom full of children.

Conversely, if your child takes longer to grasp the basic skills involved in reading, writing, or math computation, you can take as long as is necessary to make sure your child has mastered the basic concepts. If your child's pace is slower than the average, homeschooling prevents your child from feeling like a "failure" because he doesn't learn as rapidly as other children.

A continued passion for learning is one major benefit of moving forward as your child is ready. Because your child can move as rapidly as needed, he won't become bored. Because your child can move as slowly as needed, he won't suffer from low self-esteem because he can't match the speed of other learners.

You can match your teaching speed perfectly with your child's mastery of any given concept or skill. You won't waste instructional time on needless review, and you won't race ahead before your child has mastered the basic skills he needs.

Learning Efficiency

Learning at home is also very efficient. Aside from the perfect pacing, you will avoid the all-encompassing issue of "classroom management" that traditional teachers have to utilize.

Your child won't have to wait until a specific time to go to the bathroom, get a snack, or take a much-needed break. If your child needs to go to the bathroom, it will take a minute or two. You won't have to line up an entire class, migrate to the bathroom as a group, and take turns using the facility. Not to mention, your child will be able to focus on learning whenever he is receiving instruction, without being distracted by thoughts of needing to run to the bathroom, being hungry, etc., while waiting for the scheduled time.

Lunch can be as fast or slow as you like it. You can enjoy lunch with your child and take a long, refreshing lunch break, or you can eat lunch relatively quickly to get back to working on academics. Your child won't have to take an extended period of time lining up, migrating to a cafeteria, allowing time for everyone to get their lunch, or speed through eating lunch because he was the last one in line. Lunchtime can be whatever you want it to be.

In our family, we have long enjoyed our weekly lunch with Dad. One day per week, the boys and I would go pick up their dad at work, and have a nice lunch together as a family. I think our weekly lunch period was the favorite of just about everyone in the family!

In addition to the time that is wasted in the mechanics of traveling in lines at public school, there is the process of learning in the classroom. If your child understands the material perfectly, valuable learning time is "wasted" for your child as he waits for questions to be answered for other children. They are often questions your child does not have.

On the other end of the Q & A process in the classroom, your child may never get his questions answered, particularly if he has a lot of them. He may be too shy to ask a question or to admit he doesn't understand in front of a full classroom of children who may laugh at his lack of understanding. Thus, as a child gets older, he is less likely to ask a question when he discerns that the other children understand a concept. Therefore, your child will fail to learn well and will get further behind peers.

Statistical data has long shown that children who are homeschooled are often ahead of their traditionally schooled peers. I believe simple efficiency in learning contributes to better learning progress more than just about any other factor. For children who learn quickly, they can bolt ahead with their learning as rapidly as they are able, which puts them well ahead of their peers in typical classrooms who are waiting for everyone to gain the same level of conceptual understanding.

Homeschooled children who learn slowly also progress faster because their needs are being attended to on a one-to-one basis. The child can be taught concepts thoroughly and for full understanding, which enables the child to move forward on a solid foundation rather than a shaky one that will cause problems as the child advances in grade level.

Thus, eliminating all of the necessary classroom management; traveling in lines; and waiting for the appropriate time for lunch, the bathroom, or movement breaks saves time when homeschooling. Avoiding answering questions your child doesn't have while answering questions he does have allows your child to learn at the perfect pace for his individual needs. All of this adds up to a more efficient learning process.

Highly Tailored Instruction

One of the best things about homeschooling is the ability to tailor instruction precisely to your child's learning needs. As we touched on already, your child can move as quickly or slowly as needed, he can have all of his questions answered, and no time is wasted answering questions about material your child already understands. You can match your teaching pace perfectly with your child's learning speed, and you can provide instruction that matches your child's learning style.

Your ability to match your teaching pace to your child's learning pace probably needs little explanation. If you are working on instruction with your child, you will know if he has mastered the reading, writing, and math computation skills he needs. If he hasn't, you can simply keep working on the skills until he learns them.

Regarding learning styles, there are several learning style models, and each has its own merit. The most widely used model identifies learners as auditory (learn through language), visual (learn through imagery and demonstration), and kinesthetic (learn through experience or by doing). Your child's specific learning style is a major factor in how well he will learn from presented instruction.

It's important to note that most teachers teach in their own learning style. Most teachers are auditory learners and they teach in an auditory style by nature. These teachers like talking, they learn from books and through hearing, and they teach in a similar fashion. For a child who is a visual or kinesthetic learner, learning in a traditional classroom can be more difficult unless the teacher is one who conscientiously teaches to each learning style or if she happens to be of a different learning style her self.

When schooling at home, you are able to teach your child according to his needs. I say you are "able" to, but you have to be aware of your own tendency to teach the way you learn rather than the way your child learns. If you have the same learning style as your child, you are in luck! Your job will be easier. If your learning styles are different, it may be more difficult for you, as a teacher, to teach toward your child's learning style, but at least you have awareness and the ability to do so.

As an example, many children who don't do well in traditional classrooms are kinesthetic learners. With this learning style, the child needs to be moving, doing something, exploring or working with his hands in order to fully understand concepts. Few traditional classroom teachers regularly teach in this manner because it is difficult to manage a classroom with 20-30 elementary-aged children who are all participating in project-based learning. There is some project-based learning, probably in every classroom at some point in time, but teaching through hands-on activities does not happen every day as the primary means of instruction. Thus, children who are kinesthetic learners are more often considered hyperactive, may get into trouble more often for moving when they aren't supposed to, and the instruction will not be as effective for them.

In your homeschool, you can provide all of your instruction through project-based learning, active hands-on work, or you can allow your child to move freely while you teach him. My younger son used to flip over the arms of one of our chairs, the sofa, or slide off the sofa upside down repeatedly as I read aloud to him. If I asked him questions, he could answer them correctly; being able to move freely allowed him to learn well.

I will mention a small 'con' here: Finding instructional materials for kinesthetic learners is more difficult than it is to find materials for auditory or visual learners. It is easiest to find materials for auditory learners, who learn from language, as most curricula are provided through books. Because reading and writing are both language-based activities and processed in the language center of the brain, auditory learners benefit from a wide variety of available instructional materials.

Teaching visual learners is only slightly more difficult than teaching auditory learners. It is fairly easy to find picture-rich books such as the DK Publishing line of books, or to use educational DVDs published by National Geographic, The History Channel, Discovery Channel, etc. There are a wide variety of sources for picture-rich content in books and teaching videos, although they are usually nonfiction titles rather than specifically intended to be curricula for teaching. As such, you will have to devise your own way to measure your child's learning because the nonfiction titles don't often include teacher's manuals, workbooks, test booklets, etc.

It is most difficult to find instructional materials for kinesthetic learners. You will find materials by searching for manipulatives, projects, experiential learning, hands-on, or similar terms. Most project-based learning kits are assumed to be add-ons to traditional instruction and are often not comprehensive instruction as standalone projects. For example, it is easy to find kits to build a volcano, but the kits do not contain much in the way of instruction about how volcanoes are formed, the function of volcanoes in creating land mass or islands, specifics about lava, etc. In order to make the project a full learning experience, you would have to obtain additional teaching materials or content knowledge to teach your child as he builds the volcano. Thus, although it is a benefit to be able to teach a kinesthetic learner in his specific learning style, it will require additional research and effort on your part to formulate comprehensive learning on any given subject.

No matter what your child's learning style is, you can teach him or her with high efficiency by teaching according to your child's individual needs. It isn't always easy, but it can definitely be fun if you are able to cherish the time spent working with your child.

Benefits for Special Learning Needs

If your child has special learning needs, homeschooling provides a wide variety of possibilities. One study shows that traditional schooling focuses more on what a child can't do while homeschooling parents focus more on what a child can do. Jacque Ensign, a Ph.D. from the University of Virginia, with a background in foundations of education, observed homeschooled students' progress and concluded, "These students have not followed expected patterns for students with their classifications and they have not been taught with the same assumptions and techniques used by special educators" (Ensign, 2000, p. 147). When talking about homeschooled children, Ensign also states, "These students have good self-esteem because they have areas of expertise and are respected for what they do, rather than known for what they do not do well" (Ensign, 2000, p. 154). Notice the difference: A child's disability is the focus in traditional classroom settings, but his abilities are the focus in the homeschool environment.

Additionally, working with your child at home in a one-on-one instructional format allows you to be sure your child masters concepts and allows you to provide the precise program your child needs. Personally teaching your child each day lets you react in a highly responsive manner to your child's specific learning needs.

Learning Mastery

One of the biggest problems children with learning disabilities have in traditional classrooms is getting "left behind." They require direct, specific, explicit instruction in every detail to master basic skills in reading, writing, or math, depending upon their area of disability. Seldom does any traditional classroom have or take the time to make sure each individual child has fully grasped content before moving forward. Sadly, when a child is left behind and subsequently identified as having a learning disability (or two), the learning expectations for that child are then lowered by the school teachers and administrators. If a child is moved to a remedial class, he seldom advances well enough to be placed full-time into a typical classroom again. Thus, by the end of high school, the child may be well behind his peers, may or may not get an actual diploma, and has seldom been taught in a way that enables him to achieve his full potential in life.

Did you know that if a child has a learning disability he may be slower at learning than many children, but he has the full ability to learn? Being capable of learning is part of the clinical definition of having a learning disability. However, schools often dismiss the learning needs of students with learning disabilities as if they are unable to learn. While this is not the case in every school, by any means, it is the case in many schools. Thus, if you feel your child is capable of learning more than the school is teaching him, he probably is capable of learning more. Your child may be the ideal candidate for schooling at home because you can teach him whatever he wants to know by teaching toward his individual needs.

When teaching your learning-abled child at home, you can work on concepts to the point of mastery and automaticity. In other words, you can keep working on a concept, presenting the content in new and creative ways, until your child fully understands and remembers the concept. Mastery and automaticity are particularly critical for skills that are built on a progressive foundation of concepts, such as reading, writing, and math. For example, a child must understand the sounds letters represent before he can decode words for reading and before he can encode words for writing. Without the basic understanding of sound-symbol relationships in reading and writing, a child simply cannot read nor write effectively.

As a specific example, consider the blends "bl," "fl," and "sl." If a child does not understand the sound the letter "b" represents and the sound an "l" represents, it will be difficult for him to understand that "bl" is a blended sound from the sound of "b" and the sound of "l." If you are working one-on-one with your child, you will be able to determine if your child has mastered basic letter sounds in order to move forward into blends, short words, syllables, multi-syllable words, etc.

Homeschooling provides an ideal means for ensuring your child has reached concept mastery, which will build a firm foundation for more advanced learning in the upper grades. You can be certain your child has a firm foundation of the basics before advancing his learning to the next concept.

Special Program Provisioning

One of the most frustrating aspects of having a child with special needs in a public school is when you know what your child needs, but you can't convince the school to provide the needed instruction. Even when a parent provides the school with a comprehensive neuro-psychological evaluation that specifies precisely what a child needs, if the school district doesn't agree or doesn't want to provide the program—they won't! If a child is not doing well in whatever program the school is providing, it is up to the parents to force the school to provide the program recommended by the evaluator. That requires a lot of money and time, and forcing the issue builds ill-will with the school.

In fact, even if you win the court case and the school has to provide the needed instructional program, you can't make them provide the program properly without suing again. This was the precise scenario we faced with our public school. In hindsight, we regretted spending even a minute and a dime trying to get the school to teach our son properly. With time, it became evident they either couldn't or wouldn't teach him well.

Through homeschooling, you can provide the precise program your child needs without having to convince your school to provide the appropriate program. It may cost you extra money to hire a private provider or to acquire the needed instructional materials yourself. If you are going to provide the program for your child, you may need training, but it can be well worth the money and effort when compared with trying to force the school to meet your child's specific needs. There is immeasurable cost in the impact on your child's life if he does not receive instruction that is able to meet his individual needs, so I recommend you do whatever you can to ensure your child gets an appropriate education.

For us, homeschooling provided a dramatic difference in our older son's learning progress and achievement. If we had put the money toward our son's education from the beginning rather than trying to convince our school to do their job properly, our son would have been spared the dramatic impact on his self-esteem that he suffered in being treated like he was unable to learn from second grade through fourth grade. Once we brought him home and started meeting his specific needs properly, he began progressing well in his learning. He is now in college on an honors scholarship. We had a great outcome for our child whom the school said would never learn to read well!

Responsive Instruction

In addition to being able to provide the specific type of instruction your child needs, you can change your rate of teaching dynamically. You can slow down instruction whenever needed and speed up when your child exhibits good learning progress.

You can change or adjust your program at the first hint it isn't working. Schools typically put a child's remedial program in place for the entirety of the school year, seldom making meaningful adjustments or changes without a formal review, meetings, testing, and changing of a child's Individual Education Plan (IEP). The time it takes for a public school to modify their program can be months or even an entire school year. If the program is proving ineffective, that means a child will lose weeks, months, or an entire school year of meaningful educational progress.

As a homeschooling parent, you can change the rate of teaching in your program, modify teaching methods, or even switch the entire program based upon your child's individual needs. Responsiveness to your child's individual needs can mean there is little to no wasted time providing ineffective instruction. While there may be a short period of wasted instruction between the time you implement a program and seeing the evidence a program isn't working, you can modify the program as soon as you determine a change is needed. You don't have to go through bureaucratic channels to prove a program isn't working or to determine what changes are needed. You can seek out resources and information for making a change at any time.

Sometimes the process of finding the right program can prove frustrating, and you may need to seek outside input to find viable solutions. The Learning Abled Kids' support group is an excellent place to ask questions regarding programs that may provide the specific type of instruction your child needs. We have over 1600 members who help

support each other as we all work to meet our child's needs through homeschooling. You can find the Learning Abled Kids support group at:
http://groups.yahoo.com/neo/groups/LearningAbledKids/.

Benefits for Advanced Learning Needs

If your child is a speedy learner, homeschooling allows your child to learn as fast and furious as he wants to learn! There is nothing to hold your child back. If your child is given free-reign in the library, given comprehensive educational resources, and has access to Internet-based learning tools, he can teach his self at a faster pace than traditional schooling allows. Because your child is not constrained to a regimented lesson plan, he can move through content as fast as he wishes.

Learning Advancement

Parents of advanced learners may be concerned that their child's level of needed instruction will surpass the parents' level of knowledge, but these days there are many ways to provide learning opportunities for your child without needing to know the content yourself.

As an example, I've never studied physics. I knew nothing about it, and I didn't feel at all prepared to teach the topic to my boys. My older son, who is a very self-motivated learner, pretty much taught physics to himself. I had possession of the answer book for all of the problems and exams, but I could offer no assistance other than whether he had obtained the correct answer or not. Being a diligent soul who loves learning, he was determined to figure it all out, so he studied, read a lot, watched instructional videos online, etc. Through his efforts, he was able to gain a full understanding of physics and scored very well on the unit exams. He passed his physics course in college with no difficulty whatsoever.

My younger son, who has never loved school or studying, was advanced in his studies and wanted to take physics as a foundational course for his college preparation. However, he is not a driven learner like his brother, so when he failed to fully grasp a concept, he required more involvement from an instructor who could direct and teach him. I found an individual who offered an honors physics course online, signed my son up for the course, and the study of physics commenced. My son was able to call his instructor anytime he needed to, correspond with him via e-mail, and he completed the course with a fabulous grade.

For any course your child needs, you can probably find an online course, a dual-enrollment course, a local teacher, or some other avenue to meet your child's learning needs. I still don't know physics, and I am thankful I don't have to "know it all" in order for my guys to learn advanced topics.

Advanced Avenues of Study

There are many avenues for advanced learning which your child can take advantage of if he is homeschooled. Both of my boys finished high school with their freshman year of college already behind them. They left home and went to college as college sophomores.

Consider for a moment that typical public schools must teach for a regimented number of days and for a specific number of hours. Given any textbook, the school basically divides the content to be covered that school year into equally distributed units to make the teaching last for the entirety of the school year. Here in Georgia, the accrediting agency requires 150 hours of study in a topic in order for the student to get credit for a core academic subject.

What if your child can finish his history textbook in 90 hours? Accrediting agencies do not account for rapid learning in their rules. Your child must "study" that subject for 150 hours even if that means sitting in the classroom doing nothing because he has already mastered the content. Thus, the extra "study" time is just wasted time with no meaningful educational progress. Now, a lot of schools do provide advanced classes that work at a more rapid pace, but there again, the pace is at a predetermined rate regardless of your child's ability to learn faster.

With homeschooling, your child can finish the subject in 90 hours and you can move on to the next course or more advanced content. For many homeschooled children, finishing content early either provides shorter school days that allow for the pursuit of passionate interests, or it provides the opportunity to zoom ahead academically. Ours has been a bit of both, but both of my guys decided they wanted to advance academically to finish their schooling, including college, as soon as feasible.

If your child is an advanced-pace learner, there are many avenues for advanced avenues of study. Whether or not your child wishes to gain college credit for his studies will determine what avenue your child takes for his advanced learning.

If your child does not care about obtaining early college credit, open university opportunities are great for advanced studies. The following are open courses available for free online:

- MIT's Open Course initiative - http://ocw.mit.edu/index.htm
- Open Yale - http://oyc.yale.edu/courses
- Harvard Open Learning Initiative - http://www.extension.harvard.edu/open-learning-initiative

Basically, these universities put their lecture materials, notes, and videos online and allow open access to anyone, which provides a great learning opportunity for anyone who wants to take advantage of the courses. All you have to do is acquire the associated textbook and follow the teaching syllabus provided with the course materials. A person can gain a lot of knowledge at the college level this way without worrying about the cost, location, grades, etc. If a person is a self-driven learner, the open university initiatives are among the best educational opportunities available for advanced learning.

If your child wants to obtain college credit simultaneously with high school credit, you can take advantage of programs such as CLEP (College Level Examination Program), dual enrollment at a college or online, and community college classes. The avenue that will suit your child best will depend upon his ability to do well on exams or function in a traditional classroom.

The CLEP program provides a means for obtaining college credit through examination. Before going this route, you would want to consider two things: (1) Is your child good at taking exams? and (2) Does the college your child wants to attend give credit for CLEP examinations?

My older son obtained most of his advanced credit through the CLEP program. Whenever he studied a high school subject, like biology, he could finish it in less than a typical school year. He would then embark on more advanced study of the subject to cover material taught in a typical freshman college class. At the end of his advanced studies, we would go to our nearest university and he would take the CLEP exam, obtain a passing score, and thereby gain CLEP credit. My son took CLEP exams for biology, chemistry, US history, world history, analyzing and interpreting literature, college algebra, and pre-calculus.

When it came time for him to apply to and attend college, he would not consider any college that did NOT give credit for passing CLEP exams. Thus, he began college ranked as a sophomore with 39 credit hours, about two-thirds of which was obtained via CLEP. The other portion was obtained through dual-enrollment courses.

My younger son is not a stellar test-taker. Although he passed one CLEP exam, he hates testing and preferred not to go that route. Therefore, he chose to gain advanced credit primarily through dual-enrollment courses online. Because he is also not a proficient note-taker, taking classes online allows him to work at his own pace and alleviates his need to take notes. Some of his classes have been through Marshall University's Online College Classes for High School Students (http://www.marshall.edu/occhs/) and Georgia Perimeter Online (http://www.gpc.edu/online/). Because his coursework is through accredited university programs, it is accepted at any college he may attend. This provides greater flexibility in his destination college than CLEP exams would provide. My younger son graduated from high school with 36 college credit hours, making him a sophomore when he moved to the college campus.

If your child likes being with peers, wants to be in a typical classroom, and has no trouble taking notes, then having your child attend a local technical school, college, or university is a great option too. As with the online dual-enrollment programs, coursework obtained through a regionally accredited college or university will be accepted at any similarly accredited college your child may choose to attend.

Being able to complete advanced studies is also cost-effective as many programs designed for jointly enrolled high school students are offered at a reduced cost when compared to full-tuition, full-time college programs. The ability to complete advanced studies while in high school is one of the greatest benefits for anyone who learns at an advanced pace.

Special Interest Explorations

If your child finishes his schoolwork rapidly each day, this will leave time for him to pursue passions. Many homeschoolers we know pursue dance, sports, drama, art, or other interests to a level of mastery beyond peers in public school. Because your child can finish all of his schoolwork during his school day, there is no "homework," or as my son says, "It is all homework!" This leaves extra time for practice, competition, etc.

While my older son was in public school, his slower working speed meant he often had a lot of extra work to complete at the end of the school day. He had both homework and school work to complete in the evenings; therefore, he had no available time to pursue other interests. His life was pretty much sleeping, going to school, and doing homework.

Once we began homeschooling, he would work during the day on his studies. With the individual attention, extra time on task, and his active engagement in learning, he finished his work each day in a much shorter time frame than I had anticipated before we began homeschooling. Having no homework left an open window for my son to pursue outside activities, which turned out to be a huge key in rebuilding his self-esteem which was demolished while he was in public school.

My son decided he'd like to learn how to kayak. We signed up for a local homeschool kayak program, he learned to paddle and to sprint, and he even won some medals in kayak races. Kayaking gave him a sense of accomplishment that academics had not yet provided. As such, my son saved up his money, bought his own kayak, and kayaking will forever be a lifelong passion of his. If it hadn't been for homeschooling, he would never have had the opportunity to participate in the kayak program.

Thus, efficiency in learning can allow time for your child to find new interests or to practice his current interests to perfection. Either way, the extra time for special interests is also a great avenue to socialization for homeschooled children. A child's interests allow him or her the opportunity to connect with people who have similar interests and to develop meaningful relationships with other children.

2 PATIENCE IS A VIRTUE

The number one thing people say to me when they find out I homeschool my children is, "I could never do that! I don't have enough patience!" Believe me, I did not have much patience going into homeschooling, but the circumstances of homeschooling changed our household dynamics so that patience became much less of an issue. I really was surprised by how much our household dynamics changed within six months of beginning homeschooling such that we were all happy to be together all the time.

Public School Demands

The lifestyle driven by the public school's calendar is stressful by nature. Your child goes to school, comes home, and says, "I have to make a poster for Mrs. Best's class, I have to write an essay for Mrs. Hurt's class, I have two pages of math problems to work, and we have a test in Mrs. Jones' class tomorrow." Right away, you see that you have to go to the store to get some poster board, you know your child will take at least a couple of hours for his essay, he'll probably struggle with the math worksheets, and he needs to study for his test. Oh, and tonight you happen to have your son's soccer game right after dinner. Are you stressed out? You bet you are! Chances are your child is feeling stressed out too.

One of the biggest stresses in dealing with a traditional school is that you do not make the plans and you are not in control of your children's schedule. The teachers will assign homework regardless of any activities your child may have, and each teacher assigns work without any coordination with other teachers. Often it seems like weeks are all-or-nothing: either there is so much scheduled you don't see how anyone in your family will survive, or you have so little going on that everyone feels like they have nothing to do.

With traditional schooling, there is no consideration for your child's workload or the time he needs to complete assignments in relation to everything else going on. Because your child may be stressed out about everything he has due, he may exhibit feelings of anger or frustration, or he may be whiny or may procrastinate.

As the parent, you know your child has to get his work done, regardless of how unreasonable the load is, so you push your child to get his work done and the workload becomes a tug-of-war. You are pressing every moment to accomplish something, and your child is on the verge of shutting down his brain because he is overloaded, so you experience a clash of tempers driven by the stress of being in a situation you can't control.

When you homeschool, you are in charge of how much work is done each day. You know your child's working speed as well as his scheduled activities. You are capable of adjusting your child's schoolwork on a daily basis to match his activities schedule and to enable your child to reasonably manage his schoolwork. You have no end-of-the-day surprises where you have to run to the store for poster board, or make cupcakes to bring to a party, or buy supplies for an art project, etc. You know when the art projects are scheduled, so you can plan ahead.

The removal of surprises and a highly variable homework load reduces stress naturally. When you remove the stress factors, it becomes a whole lot easier to be patient on a daily basis. If you aren't stressed out and your kids aren't pushed to the breaking point, then everyone can talk a lot more calmly and amicably, and you can problem solve any issues that come up without a lot of drama. The bottom line is with homeschooling, you are put back into control of your family life on a daily basis.

Traditional schools are driven by calendars that don't match your family's desired timing for activities, events, or special circumstances. When homeschooling, you might have a schooling-based emergency or surprise from time to time, but they will be rare occurrences. Thus, you will likely be a lot more relaxed on a daily basis. You will find your family life becomes calm when compared to the storms neighboring families are experiencing. You will be at the helm of your ship, and they will be tossed upon the waves and whims of their school system.

Long Day + Homework

Along with the scheduling surprises and stresses created by public schools, if your child is in a traditional school, there is added stress from being on an artificial schedule. You and your child are raked out of bed early in the morning to get ready for and to catch the school bus. Your child is run through the mill all day at school, and by time your child gets home, he just wants to chill, but he has homework. A tired child with homework demands makes for avoidance, frustration, and anger.

As discussed in the prior section, the scenario above results in a lot of stress. If you repeat the cycle day after day, month after month, as occurs with public school, you end up with a tired, frazzled, and non-compliant child. On top of that, you are tired, just wishing for a break, and you are thankful for those weeks when your child does not have homework.

What is the good news? With homeschooling, there is no homework. Can you imagine? Every single evening is family time, open for activities, or available to do whatever you wish to do. Your child can relax and go to bed at a natural time that suits him. He can get up in the morning whenever he wakes and is ready to get up.

Given a full night's sleep without having to stay up late to do homework or get up early to catch a bus, your child will be well rested. A fully rested child will be more alert and able to be actively engaged in his learning each day. You can schedule your school day to start at your child's optimal learning time.

No longer will you have an arbitrary, regimented schedule dictating what time you go to bed, get up, or study. With biologically driven, need-based sleeping and waking, no homework, and no scheduling surprises, you will have much less stress and a happier family!

Having a happier family makes it a lot easier to exercise patience than you can probably imagine. Reducing our stress simply by getting away from the school's calendar and onto our own schedule probably had the greatest impact on our stress levels and our ability to exercise patience with each other. It was a surprising change of dynamics, which I'm sure you will love more than you can imagine.

Artificial Learning Speeds

Along with the stresses of the public school calendar and unexpected assignments, the schools follow a certain expected learning path regardless of the speed at which your individual child learns. Each day's lessons in school include the message: Learn this NOW! The public school has to teach the specified content on a given day whether a child is ready to learn it or not.

For children with learning struggles, the more hurried the class is in school, the further behind a slow-speed learner gets. Those who learn more slowly need more time to grasp concepts. If a child learns slowly, there simply is not enough time to address his individual needs during the school day, which often means the child is completing the day's schoolwork as homework in addition to having the regularly scheduled homework. Therefore, as mentioned earlier in the book: a child who struggles ends up going to school, doing homework, and sleeping, in a cycle of trying to catch up that never seems to end. Such a life is no life for a child.

Children who are homeschooled don't have to be pressured to do more than they're capable of at any given moment. In fact, a lot of families choose a more relaxed-paced, year-round schooling model to keep their learner progressing on grade level but at a manageable pace. As we talked about in the first chapter, a child who takes longer to do his schoolwork can benefit from cutting out all of the inefficiencies in a public school day too, which enables the child to complete schoolwork during the day and to have time for relaxation or activities in the evening.

For advanced learners, they're ready to learn something new, but they often have to complete tedious worksheets. This type of "busy work" annoys them, and the boredom in the classroom can lead to discipline problems. The tediousness of their traditional schooling experience can lead to school hatred or disinterest, both of which are frustrating for parents. As a parent, you know if your child is capable but just won't do his homework, and your awareness of your child's capabilities can lead to frustration and loss of patience on your part.

The artificial holding back of a student so that he can keep pace with the average speed of learning can have harmful effects aside from just limiting the speed of learning. The resentment, boredom, and other psychological factors create bad attitudes about school which parents see developing in their teens. If a teen views going to school as a waste of his time, his bad attitude is exhibited regularly. However, if the child can learn as fast as he wants and engage in meaningful learning experiences, then a bad attitude will disappear. You will easily have more patience with a child who is happy. Patience with rapidly advancing learners becomes a non-issue when the child doesn't have to engage in meaningless busy work day after day. They can do one lesson, master it, and move on!

Thus removal of the artificial learning speed in schooling can help the psyche of any child. As a parent, patience becomes more evident with homeschooling because you avoid the frustration of dealing with school circumstances you cannot change coupled with a child who hates school for one reason or another. When homeschooling, you are in charge of your child's day, so you can adjust it to fit his individual needs and your needs, which invariably makes for a much better scenario for everyone involved.

Simply put, if you are not in control of your child's schooling and your child is stressed out, you will be too. If you are in control and can make changes as needed, you and your child can work together to find what works best for him or her. Working together builds bonds in your parent-child relationship. You are empowered by being in control of your family life, and that goes a long way toward enabling you to exercise greater patience than might seem possible at this moment in time.

Let's Call It What It Is

There are two additional factors which cause bad attitudes and stress within a household, and which might be counterproductive for homeschooling. There are potential temperamental issues with children and parents which need to be considered prior to making a decision to homeschool. These areas of concern aren't easy to talk about, so I think it is best to just be blunt and call it like it is. I'm sure you'll be able to comprehend these issues, and hopefully the thoughts will help provide direction in your decision-making.

Dealing with Bratty Attitudes

First, a major factor to consider when deciding whether to homeschool is your own kids' degree of sassiness, angry attitudes, etc. When your child goes to public school all day, every day, there is often an unfortunate assimilation of an attitude that comes from being within the peer-driven environment day after day. Sometimes the attitude is one of anger toward parents, anger toward adults in general, defiance, or general disrespect.

I'm not entirely sure what the social dynamics are which lead to the adoption of bratty attitudes, but I have seen the attitude develop in a significant number of children (not all) who go to public school. The attitude is more pervasive among teens that are in traditional school environments than it is among homeschooled students. Some of the attitude seems to stem from the child feeling as if adults just don't care about him, some comes from constant stress at school, and a lot of the attitude seems to come from the social culture among teens who think it is "cool" to be full of themselves and arrogant toward authority figures.

You might find it hard to believe, but it doesn't have to be that way, and, with homeschooling, unless the bratty attitude is severe, it general diminishes over time given a patient, loving parent guiding the child at home. If homeschooling begins early enough, the attitude may never develop at all.

This isn't to say there aren't bratty homeschooled children because there are a few. It also isn't to say that there aren't perfectly wonderful, respectful children in public school. There are probably more wonderful children in public school, relatively speaking, than there are bratty homeschoolers, but the proportional balance is much more in favor of happy, positive attitudes among homeschooled children.

While I'm not entirely sure why the social dynamics at public schools lead to haughty attitudes and subsequent clashes with parents, I can explain several factors that play into better attitudes among homeschooled children.

Among the masses at public school, there is a culture among students where it is often more socially acceptable to be defiant toward authority figures such as teachers and parents. In homeschools, the kids don't observe or adopt the attitudes of other kids at school. With a parent as the homeschool teacher, the parent can correct bad behaviors and bad attitudes as soon as they might be evidenced, which helps keep sassy attitudes from developing into a bad habit when addressed properly from an early age.

There is also an attitude of disregard for schoolwork among many students in public school. Some of this stems from the advanced learners who think the work is all busy work, and some of it stems from children who are struggling and want to seem strong by saying the schoolwork is dumb. Bad attitudes toward schoolwork often come from a learning environment and learning speed that do not match the needs of the child.

With homeschooling, a child doesn't have to do extra work to prove he has learned something. Once he has learned it, he can move on. There is no need to save face among peers, so a child who is struggling doesn't have to pretend to be cooler than the schoolwork to show he is somebody valuable. The homeschooled child is the only student in his class and is right on time with his learning. He doesn't have to prove anything to his peers, so that helps prevent bad attitudes from developing toward schoolwork.

Another attitude issue stems from the bullying and belittling some children suffer at the hands of other kids. The smart kids are teased for being smart. The slow learners are teased for being slow. Fat kids are teased, poor kids are teased, awkward kids are teased, etc. For every child that is teased, the child's self-esteem is damaged. Over time, the diminishing of the child's self worth can lead to anger, depression, resentment, frustration, or a whole host of other emotions. Let's face it: There are a lot of teasers, a lot of kids who are teased, and therefore a lot of bad attitudes running around a school that stem from a child being treated badly.

If your child's mindset is different from the collective mindset about what is cool in school, he is likely to have been teased and bullied in school. Thus, he may have developed an attitude as a means of self-protection and as a way to hide his pain. This is the easiest kind of attitude to get away from. Simply by bringing your child home, treating him with love and respect, valuing him as a person, and teaching him as a capable learner, you will help build his self-esteem back to a level where the attitude is no longer needed as a shield for hurt feelings.

Whatever your child's attitude may be, you need to consider its causes and possible solutions. If your child's brattiness is beyond your ability to cope with the attitude, I'd suggest seeking professional help or investing in a top-notch behavior intervention type of program to help you develop a better working relationship with your child before you actually begin homeschooling. Although homeschooling is likely to improve attitudes for all of the reasons mentioned so far, if your child is highly defiant and angry, it would be difficult to add homeschooling on top of the attitude issues.

Given significant attitude problems, it is entirely possible your child is crying out for help and support, so please do not let the attitude alone stop you. With the thought toward developing a mutually loving, beneficial relationship with your child, getting professional help followed by homeschooling could be exactly what you need to help turn your relationship with your child around.

The Parent Side of the Patience Equation

On the parental side, I think it is best to be blunt here. I think there are parents who should not homeschool their children. If you are such a parent, I'd like to think you know who you are. Truly, if you know yourself, you know who you are capable of becoming and whether you are capable of being with your children 24 hours per day, 7 days per week without wanting to smack them around. If you are a parent whose temper gets the best of you and you physically discipline your children in a state of anger, then you could very well be pushed to the brink of intolerance by homeschooling. Thus, until you can put away anger-driven physical punishment forever and use talking, timeouts, removal of privileges, and other non-physical means for discipline, you probably should not homeschool your children.

That said, if your impatience comes in the form of screaming at your children on occasion, feeling totally exasperated with them, wanting to tear your hair out (but you don't actually tear it out), then you may find yourself pleasantly surprised by how much less of a problem daily stresses are once you are established with homeschooling.

Considering the factors we already discussed about how homeschooling changes dynamics within the home, there is a good possibility that many of your historical problem areas will no longer be a significant issue. I'll let you know too that I felt uncertain about my own temperament before we began, but things were better than I ever hoped they would be once our homeschooling became routine.

So, how do you know if you have enough patience to homeschool aside from whatever drama might be instilled in your home at this moment? A degree of honest self-reflection is helpful. These points of reflection are based upon areas which I believe are key factors in coping from my personal experience and observation of other homeschooling parents. When considering your answers to the questions, be totally honest with yourself. No one else is going to know your answers or judge you based upon your thoughts or feelings. In the long run, it will be better for your family, yourself, and your kids if you know yourself first. When thinking about your patience level, consider:

● When your children were little, before they ever went to school, did you love spending time with them? --OR-- Were you so stressed by parenting responsibilities that you couldn't wait for them to start school so that you could have a break? I've known parents on both ends of this spectrum. Your ability to tolerate being around kids all the time has more to do with your personal ability to cope with the stress of dealing with kids than it does your level of love for your children.

● Do you look forward to summertime and enjoy school holidays with your kids? --OR-- Do you yearn for summer vacation to be over so that you can send your kids back to school? Tolerance for being with your kids is probably the most significant factor when considering homeschooling.

● Do you have a love and passion for your kids above all else besides possibly God and your spouse? --OR-- Are you more interested in your career, hobbies, or other aspects of self-development? While I think everyone has an interest in their own self-development, homeschooling does require that the homeschooling parent put his or her children before everything else on a daily basis. This is more true in the elementary years than in high school because mid- to upper-teens are often able to work independently much of the time, which frees a parent to pursue her interests to a degree. The demands of homeschooling generally dictate that the children's needs are of the highest priority.

If you can honestly see that you are willing to make your children your highest priority, and you earnestly want to provide them with the best educational opportunity you are capable of providing, then you can probably exercise or develop sufficient patience to deal with your children each and every day. This does not mean you will be perfect and never lose your temper, never yell at your kids or feel exasperated, but rather that you will be sufficiently able to cope and that you will not become a screaming banshee!

I'm betting the change in dynamics which comes with homeschooling will be sufficient to enable you to cope without losing your cool as it did for me. Coping was the most difficult for the first three to five months of homeschooling after my guys had been in public school for three and five years. We had to spend a period of time reframing expectations—both mine and my boys.

Given my older son had become convinced he could not learn, he would refuse to even try to read. He had tantrums over reading which exercised my patience on a daily basis. I had to remind myself daily about why we were homeschooling in order for me to make it through the initial months of stress. Sometimes I wondered if I had somehow made a terrible choice in deciding to homeschool. One key I held onto, which might be a good one for you to grasp right now: You can always change your mind and stop homeschooling if it doesn't work for you. That is a huge point to remember. If you have any doubts, you can always give it a whirl and change your mind later if it turns into a disaster. However, if you stick with it long enough to get past the initial adjustment period, you may be able to toss that key away forever.

With my initial stress level, it was helpful to make a note for myself to remind me why I began homeschooling. You might find making a note for yourself helpful as well. On those days when stress seems to be getting the better of you, you can go read your note to yourself and dive back into homeschooling with new hope and determination. Many times I would go shut myself in my room, cry a bit, and then I'd remember my notes about why I was homeschooling. Pulling the notes out to read them went a long way toward maintaining my determination and patience.

As an example of what you may want to write for yourself, here is my list:

1. I only have one chance to raise my boys, so I will do the best job I know how to do.

2. I want my guys to know I love them beyond a shadow of doubt.

3. My boys deserve a quality education, and I will make sure they get it.

4. My boys will make better educational progress at home than they did in public school.

5. I will not let my children grow up to be illiterate.

6. I was young once and needed patience, so I will exercise the same measure of patience I needed with my boys.

For me, patience did not seem natural when we started homeschooling, but the final point on my list always reminded me that every child wants a patient, loving parent. I aimed to be that parent my boys could look up to. I won't kid you and say it was easy because it wasn't, but it was worthwhile to exercise my patience daily. Now my friends tell me I'm more patient than anybody they know. Given my lack of patience before homeschooling and where I am today, I believe anybody—YOU—can likewise develop much greater patience than you might readily believe.

SANDRA K. COOK

3 THE "S" WORD - SOCIALIZATION

Questions abound about the socialization of children who are homeschooled. Everyone is concerned about the big "S" word. People wonder if homeschooled children will have any friends, or whether they will grow up to be socially inept or awkward. Plus, there is an assumption that the socialization children experience through public school is good.

While there is a lot of concern about socialization, virtually everything one worries about in conjunction with the socialization of homeschooled children is based upon misconceptions, misinformation, or isolated incidents with families who would operate outside of societal norms even if their kids were in public school. Let's look at the fears and the facts as they pertain to homeschooling and socialization.

Peers

The biggest fear for homeschooled children is that they will be unable to relate to their peers, will not have friends, or that they will otherwise be unable to interact with people in a normal way.

Consider this: How many of your daily interactions with people are solely with people of your own birth year? We're not considering interactions with people who are a year or two older or a year or two younger, but specifically people who were born within a few months of your birthday. In society, it would be very odd to section people at work by their birth year and allow you to interact only with persons your same age. This artificial constraint would limit your understanding of people and society across a broader range of ages.

In traditional schools, children are placed in grades artificially constrained by the child's birth date and an arbitrary cut-off day on a school calendar. Every student is taught the same thing as everyone else of the same age primarily because it is a convenient way to manage a large number of students. Students are not grouped that way because there is any inherent special socialization that occurs when grouping children in such a manner. Sectioning off children into narrow bands of same-age peers does not make them better able to interact with society at large. In fact, sectioning off children in this way does just the opposite—it restricts their ability to practice interacting with a wide variety of people.

So why do we worry about homeschooled children's socialization? The erroneous assumption is that the child will be homeschooled and will be at home, schooling in the house, all day every day, with no interactions with other people. Unless a family is remotely located in a desolate place away from any form of civilization, social isolation is highly unlikely.

Every homeschooling family I know involves their children in daily life—going to the grocery store or the bank, running errands, volunteering in the community, or participating in sports, arts, or community classes. Within the homeschooled community, sports, arts, drama, co-op classes, etc., are usually sectioned by elementary, pre-teen, and teen groupings. This allows students to interact with a wider range of children, and the interactions usually enhance a child's ability to interact well with a wider age-range of students.

Additionally, being out in the community provides many opportunities for children to interact with people of all ages. When homeschooling groups plan field trips, there are sometimes constraints on the age range, depending upon the destination, but many times the trip is open to children of all ages. As an example, when our group went on a field trip to the Federal Reserve Bank, all ages of children attended. The tour and information were of interest to all of the children in one way or another. After the tour, our group dined at a nearby food court. The parents sat together to chat and the children all sat with each other, with kids of all ages talking and having fun with each other. When interacting with society, exposure to a wider variety of people makes for better overall socialization.

Many homeschooling groups also have park days, game days, or play days that allow all of the children in the homeschooled community to come together and play. Usually such social opportunities last for two, three, or four hours. Our group used to have Friday afternoon "Park Day." After our morning studies, we would pack a picnic lunch, drive to the park, and spend the rest of the afternoon letting the kids run and play. Older kids would organize games and play with younger kids, which let them practice great leadership skills. The younger kids truly looked up to and enjoyed being included in games with the older kids.

Because parents are always present, siblings, as well as older and younger children all took care to play nicely with each other the majority of the time. Behaviors like bullying, teasing, or the excluding of any child just didn't happen.

Exclusion only occurred when a child was new to homeschooling and excluded his self because he didn't feel fully socialized into the homeschooling community yet. When a child is new to homeschooling and makes a comment about excluding someone or teases someone, he will usually be told by the other kids, "That isn't nice. She can play too," and over time the new child becomes just as inclusive as the other homeschooled children.

In public school, lunch and recess are really the only times during the school day when the children are allowed to interact with each other with a relative degree of freedom. These are usually short periods of time that don't allow for a lot of interaction, but because the kids are free to talk, it is a good time for them to connect with others. The children can certainly build lasting friendships with other children during lunchtime at school, but lunchtime and recess interactions do not equate to "better" socialization in the grander scale of life.

One of the other things I like about homeschool socialization is the fluidity of a child's ability to self-select his friend group. We all know children who are a little bit socially immature or those children who are very serious and interact better with people who are chronologically older. Given no artificial constraints built into the majority of all homeschool social opportunities, children naturally gravitate toward hanging out with the kids that are at a relatively similar level of social communication and interaction. There is virtually no tendency for the children to judge one another based upon the ages of a child's closest friends.

Thus, if a child is a bit socially immature, he may choose to hang out with children who are one or two years younger. Being the oldest in the group is beneficial because parents can see leadership skills emerge as the oldest child is looked up to as a leader by the slightly younger children. This, in turn, helps the child mature in his leadership abilities, which can enable him to interact better with same-aged peers.

If a child is serious and wants to talk about advanced topics, he can join in discussion with a group of older kids. Often, the older children will encourage the younger child and will take the opportunity to teach him new concepts. In this scenario, the children have a win-win situation where the younger child gets to learn as much as he is able and the older children learn teaching skills.

Within our homeschool community, we also have a handful of children who are significantly mentally impaired in their learning ability, but it doesn't matter. They are delightful, loving members of our group and are readily included in activities by children of all ages.

The only type of child I have seen shunned by the overall group of homeschooled children is a child who is mean-spirited and does not relent even when asked to stop. Although I would love it if our group was all-inclusive all of the time, I'd venture to guess those individuals who are mean to other people all of the time would not be well tolerated in any social group. In such a case, the child needs constant work and coaching toward appropriate social interactions. The homeschooled community of kids is likely to give the person a fair effort at inclusion. If the individual child is truly working to overcome issues, he could probably eventually fit in.

Shedding Negativity

When considering those who don't fit in, let's talk about the likelihood your child will be accepted into the group of homeschooled children as compared with how socialization goes in public school. A lot of parents consider homeschooling because of the bullying or belittling their child faces in the public school setting.

If a child has any differences, whether learning, social, race, or religion, he may be subject to meanness from other children. In our case, my older son was bullied from the very beginning of his schooling. With his executive planning difficulties, he was challenged to get the timing right to run and kick a ball. His slow processing speed often meant that his hands would come together to catch a ball after the ball had already passed through them. Thus, he was not an adept child when it came to ball-based sports where catching, kicking, and timing is essential. So, the kids teased him on the playground. Add my son's dyslexia to his planning and processing speed issues, and he was belittled regularly for his difficulty with reading. The other kids in the class would call him names, laugh at him, and his teacher would even tell him not to bother to attempt assignments because he "couldn't do them anyway."

Needless to say, over time the public school environment devastated my son's self-esteem. After five years in public school, my son was depressed. He cried in the evenings after school. He wouldn't look anyone in the eye, and he hardly spoke a word to anyone. He was convinced he was incapable of learning. This was what socialization at the public school did to my child. Homeschooling allowed us to shed all of that negativity and recover his spirit so that he is now a happy, well-adjusted young man.

If you have a child who is different in any way, or bullied for any reason, I'm sure you can relate to the hurtfulness of a belittling public school experience. If saving your child's spirit and self-esteem is the primary reason you are considering homeschooling, let me say right now—GO FOR IT! The benefits and outcomes are so much better for us than I ever anticipated. My only wish was that I had been braver and taken the leap into homeschooling sooner!

Here's why: When children are not grouped together in a structured (public) school program and are truly schooled at home, social time is all about socialization, and learning time is all about learning. Thus learning differences do not come into play during homeschool social time and social interactions don't interfere with learning while you are schooling. If you truly homeschool and don't enroll your child in classes somewhere with a large group of kids, you can move away from the learning-based judgments, negative commentary, and stigmas of being a student who learns slowly.

If your child is physically awkward or a highly gifted learner, self-consciousness and teasing can be left behind too. Because homeschooled children primarily study academics at home, none of the kids really know who is ahead, who is behind, or who is good at reading, writing, or doing math aside from telling each other, "I'm good at math." There is no comparison of one child to another among the children so that each child is accepted at face value for being the individual that he or she is.

One of the greatest benefits we found in homeschooling was the inclusiveness of the groups in activities and play and how little it mattered that my son had dyslexia. My older son was teased in public school because of his reading difficulty, and he had become downtrodden and shy. When we began homeschooling, he would not talk to the other kids. However, my son was regularly encouraged to join group activities. Because the children didn't know of his learning struggles, they encouraged him to participate in hide and seek, to go exploring in the creek, to play Simon Says or Red Rover, etc. just like every other child. The established community of homeschooled children included him—always. After a time, my son began opening up and interacting with the other children more and more, and he eventually left his self-consciousness behind.

If I consider the difference in the socialization of my son when comparing his experience in public school with his experience while being homeschooled, the winner is homeschooling without a doubt. While the form of socialization that took place in public school demolished my son's self-esteem, over a period of years my son was able to recover through the constant, ongoing encouragement of the other homeschooled children. Had I known sooner the difference it would make for my son, I would have taken the plunge into homeschooling at the first hint of social trouble in public school.

Family, Friends, and Nosey Neighbors

When deciding whether to homeschool, you will run into family members, friends, and neighbors who think you're crazy or incapable, and others who will think you're a saint. Everyone you ask will be willing to share their opinions—both good and bad—about homeschooling.

Opinions about homeschooling are usually fairly strong. However, when people share their opinions with you, always consider whether the person has any firsthand experience with homeschooling. Unless they've actually homeschooled their own children, they can't really tell you what it is like and their knowledge is theoretical or second-hand. To get a true feel for homeschooling, seek out the opinions of those who have or are actively homeschooling.

Everybody's Opinion

It seems as though everybody has an opinion about homeschooling. When you ask people what they think, you will get a wide variety of responses:

- "Homeschooling is a great idea."
- "More power to you, but I could never do that."
- "It'd drive me crazy; you must be crazy."
- "Are you sure you're qualified?"
- "How are you going to do that? You're not a teacher."
- And the most negative of all, "Nobody should homeschool their children."

Chances are you will hear most of these responses from people who have never actually homeschooled, except for maybe the first opinion on the list.

The best source for information about homeschooling is other homeschoolers. They are the only people who can truly convey what homeschooling is like on a daily basis, share with you the homeschooling resources in and around your community, and inform you about the strength of the homeschooling community in your area. No matter what your friends and relatives may feel about homeschooling, their opinions are just their opinions unless they have actually homeschooled themselves.

Thus, if you are wondering if your area has enough activities for homeschoolers, what kinds of social opportunities homeschooled children may have nearby, or if the local area has any homeschool groups, the best people to ask are other homeschoolers. Because each community has a different level of support for homeschooling, finding social activities and opportunities in your area will require you to connect with local homeschoolers. However, until you get involved in the community, it can be difficult to locate other homeschoolers.

So, let's talk about how you can ferret out the other homeschoolers in your area. Today, the Internet makes it much easier to locate other homeschoolers than it ever has been before. Using social media, you can broadcast questions such as, "Does anyone I know homeschool? Please contact me if you do. I have some questions about it." You can post announcements like this on Facebook, Twitter, or send out an e-mail blast to all of your local contacts.

Aside from asking, you can go searching. When searching, use the word "homeschool" because homeschoolers tend to write the word as a compound word whereas people who do not homeschool tend to write "home school." If you use the search term "home school" (two words), you will get results related to a public school which a student is zoned to attend—their "home school," which makes information about homeschooling more difficult to locate. The "home school" designation is not at all the same as a homeschool for which you wish to find information.

Therefore, search for "homeschool group" and your

city, county, geographic region, or state. For example, I might search for "homeschool group north Georgia." By typing in your state, region, county, or city, you will find options for local group contacts.

For information about homeschooling locally, e-mail or call the contacts for several of the groups and ask them questions about their group's activities, park days, and especially "regularly scheduled" activities. If they meet regularly one day per week or on certain days of the month, you can ask if you can come by and visit with them to see what their group is like.

Some homeschooling groups are "open," which means that any homeschooler is welcome to join in any activity with the group. Other groups may have membership requirements. There are some groups that are strictly Christian, and they sometimes require homeschoolers to sign a statement of faith. Other groups may specifically be related to homeschooling educational co-ops, so a member must be involved in their enrichment courses before participating in group activities.

For example, we have a local co-op that meets one day per week where the children receive instruction in arts, music, welding, sewing, biology (dissection), chemistry (experiments), etc. The group also holds dances and hosts field trips and social events of various kinds, but a homeschooler must be part of the co-op to participate in the co-op-sponsored social events.

When we started homeschooling, we joined an open group that met every Friday for "Park Day." From that group, we learned about all kinds of available activities for homeschoolers, and we were included in special activities scheduled by various group members. To give you an idea of the variety of available opportunities for homeschoolers, the organized activities and groups we have participated in over the past decade include:

- Tennis
- Kayaking
- Bowling
- Fencing
- Golf
- Basketball
- Drama
- Gaming Club
- Airsoft
- Park Days

- Creative Writing
- Master's Academy of Fine Arts
- First Lego League Robotics
- Odyssey of the Mind
- Middle School History Field Trips
- Homeschool Swimming
- Homeschool Skate Days
- Social Dances (casual and formal)
- Homeschool Graduation

Those were all activities specifically offered for homeschoolers during the day, usually in the afternoon, for enrichment and socialization. We participated in only a handful of opportunities available to us. There really are so many options that you have to be selective about what you spend your time participating in, otherwise you could be having social fun all the time to the detriment of academic studies.

Some of the additional opportunities which we have not personally participated in include book club, welding, jewelry making, ballet or hip hop, marching band, football, Destination Imagination, lacrosse, chorus, chess club, debate club, Mock Trial, Science Olympiad, Homeschool P.E., American Girls Club, Keepers at Home, Boy Scouts, Junior Reserve Officers Training Corps (JROTC), Geography Bee, etc. There are far too many opportunities to list. Many museums, history centers, and other venues offer homeschooling days too.

Thus, when you are inquiring about opportunities, you will want to find out about membership requirements (often these are disclosed on the groups' websites), meeting days and times, the types of events the group has, and how you can get involved. We are located in the Atlanta Metro area, so the opportunities abound here as they do in most good-sized metro areas. Any sizable city is likely to have a sizable homeschool community that you can tap into. Medium-sized cities will have some good groups and support, but they aren't likely to provide opportunities of every kind imaginable as our metro area does. If you are located within half an hour to forty-five minutes of any decently-sized city, you can probably find groups and opportunities.

That said, what do you do if you are remotely located in the countryside somewhere without any sizeable community nearby? For you, having ongoing social opportunities will be more difficult, but then I imagine they are so anyway.

When I was in school, my high school was nearly an hour's drive from my home, so I rarely got together with any friend outside of the actual school day anyway. Luckily, these days the Internet provides connect-ability with anyone in the world! Your child can have homeschooled friends who are available to chat during the day through "homeschool pen pals."

If you search that term on Google, you will find various groups that connect homeschooled children with each other. You will want to CAREFULLY SCREEN anyone you are hooking your child up with before you let the children connect. I recommend a phone call with the parent and several monitored phone calls between the children prior to connecting them up with each other independently as a minimal safety measure.

After proper screening, the use of Skype for interactive chat sessions, Google Chat, or texting back and forth can provide social interactions for your child. While it isn't quite the same thing as having other children to hang out with on a daily basis, your child will make some friends through online connections. Additionally, it won't be as though your child is totally isolated. Whatever sports, activities, church, or community happenings your child already participates in will continue to be opportunities for social interaction.

Given that your residence is remotely located, the reduction of social contact will be on a relative scale and could be more of an issue. However, given that contact is already somewhat limited, depending upon how much your child loves or doesn't love the public school experience, the impact may or may not be a detrimental factor. Only you will be able to adequately gauge how much face-to-face social interaction your child really needs to feel satisfied.

Judgment by the Clueless

Up front, negativity about homeschooling usually stems from ignorance. If a person investigates homeschooling as a viable avenue for providing education, they will find on average that homeschoolers are much more academically advanced than the average child in public school. There is an underlying assumption that a person has to be qualified to "teach" a child, but, in reality, academic engagement equals learning. If you can engage your child in learning activities, your child can learn. If you can figure out how to do hands-on projects, if you can read a book to your child, point out interesting facts, read, write, and do basic math, then you can teach your child.

Some teachers might not like me saying so, but you don't need a bachelor's degree in early childhood education with a robust understanding of child development, learning theory, and curriculum development in order to teach a child. None of the theoretical knowledge is necessary for teaching a child his colors, his numbers, his letters, his names, or any number of other things you probably already "taught" your child. In fact, much of learning takes place through active engagement with new concepts and ideas. If you expose your child to new concepts and ideas, your child will learn regardless of the presence or lack of your theoretical training in education.

It is also important for you to know there have been a few studies of homeschooled students and teaching that are enlightening to those who assume teacher training is required in order to be an effective teacher. In one of my favorite studies, it was found "homeschool students were academically engaged about two times as often as public school students and experienced more reading and math gains" (Delquadri, Duval, & Ward, 2004, p. 140). "While the students in the homeschool setting out-paced their public school counterparts," the study observes, "the low student-teacher ratio in homeschools, and not specialized training, apparently enabled parents to create effective instructional environments" (Delquadri et al., 2004, p. 153). This particular study pitted parents with high school diplomas teaching in a homeschool environment against teachers with master's degrees teaching in a small-group classroom setting.

The quoted study shows if your child is paying attention while you are working on his academic studies and you provide one-on-one attention to your child, your child will probably be able to out-pace learning that would take place in the public school setting. Whether your child is an advanced learner or a slower-paced learner, I would speculate that learning progress for your child will be better while homeschooling than it would be if your child was in public school.

This was precisely the case for my son. My older son, with his dyslexia, wasn't reading beyond a first grade level after being in public school for five years. Although he had two different "highly qualified" teachers for reading resource while he was in public school, he had not learned to read. After three years of homeschooling, his reading skills tested at a grade 12+ equivalent. I am not a "trained" teacher (although I did take a two-week, summertime course in how to teach children with dyslexia to read). Thus, teacher training isn't all it's cracked up to be, and the research shows one-on-one, actively engaged instruction is more helpful than a master's degree.

Therefore, if family members question your decision, it is good to be prepared with a combination response saying, "public school isn't meeting my kids' needs" and "one-on-one instruction is very affective for any child." Hopefully those responses will be sufficient to convince your family members that homeschooling is a viable option.

Negativity

Family members who are against homeschooling are among the most difficult to deal with. Whether you have a meddling mother, mother-in-law, sister, aunt, father, or any other family member, it is difficult to ignore their commentary. Regardless of the actual benefits of providing individualized instruction for your child, unsupportive family members may continue to doubt your ability to teach your children. Just keep in mind their opinions are only that—opinions.

Those who think you are crazy are much easier to deal with than those who sincerely believe public school is always the best option. The most difficult family members to convince are often those who are or have been public school teachers or administrators. The public school culture looks down on homeschooling, although I'm not sure why it matters to public schoolers whether anyone is homeschooled. Nevertheless, anyone who fully believes in, supports, or works in a public school can become the harshest critic. On the flip side, there are those public school personnel who will fully embrace your homeschooling because of all they see happening in the public schools. Pro-homeschooling personnel from the public school sector can also be among your staunchest of supporters.

So, how do you deal with unsupportive family members? Because they are family, they may think they have a right or duty to tell you they think your decision is wrong, and they may think they need to remind you of their opinions on a regular basis. One of the best approaches I know—and one you should take early on—is to start handing them study data and reports about successful homeschoolers. A great site for research information is the National Home Education Research Institute (http://www.nheri.org/). Statistically, it is highly unlikely your child will be more academically advanced if she goes to public school than she will be if you homeschool, but that doesn't enter into a person's thinking when they are grilling you about your decision to homeschool. Hopefully, educating your family members about the proven successes of homeschooling will allay their fears and encourage them to drop the matter from their list of concerns.

I've known families who had a lot of interference and difficulty from relatives who wouldn't relent regardless of the facts; these homeschoolers ended up having to be very firm about their decision to homeschool. Many have gone as far as telling their meddling relative the decision is final and the family member is not to bring up the subject again— ever. It can be difficult to be so blunt, but it may be necessary.

Unsupportive friends are often those who fear homeschooling themselves, or, in many cases, they are passionate supporters of public schools. Your friends are more likely to be inquisitive and ask questions, but they are far less likely to openly vocalize objections or concerns they have about your homeschooling. Thus, friends tend not to be highly problematic. Some of your friends may disagree with you heartily enough to distance themselves from you, but they usually make that choice because of their uncomfortable feelings and their inability to relate to your homeschooling lifestyle.

Nosey neighbors may wonder what you're doing, ask questions about why your kids are home, and may ask questions about your kids' well-being. Often the neighbors mean well, which is fine as long as they don't think that your homeschooling requires their supervision. There used to be a lot of interference from nosey neighbors who would call authorities when kids were not in school, but homeschooling is so pervasive now that most people understand your children are home because you are homeschooling. When faced with questions about why your kids are out of school, the simple response, "We homeschool," is an acceptable response.

Many, many times when we've been out and about on a school day, we had total strangers ask why our children were not in school, or most often they'd ask, "Is it a school holiday?" Again, we would simply say, "We homeschool." On occasion, when asked if it is a holiday, we've simply said, "Yes!" For all they know our kids are privately schooled and it is a school holiday.

Thankfully, homeschooling has become a widely accepted lifestyle. People used to homeschool primarily for religious reasons, but is no longer the case. There are homeschoolers of every kind out and about in the community, so we receive far fewer questions now than we did a decade ago.

SANDRA K. COOK

4 LONG-TERM PLANNING

Many parents are wisely concerned about the "What-ifs" of homeschooling because there can be long-term issues, depending on how long your homeschooling life lasts. It is best to consider long-term outcomes up front and to plan accordingly. One of the biggest long-term considerations is the issue of accredited versus non-accredited programs.

Elementary School

At the elementary school level, there is really very little reason to be concerned about the accreditation of any homeschool program. If you graduated from high school, there is a high probability that you are well qualified and able to teach your child the necessary foundational skills that are of primary concern in elementary school.

Should you decide to enroll or re-enroll your child into public school for any reason during elementary school, placement into a traditional classroom is usually fairly straightforward and easy. Although a school may want to administer academic skills tests to discern the level of your child's learning, there is little in the way of "placement" concerns as they pertain to elementary education.

At the elementary school level, I've never heard of any school requiring a child to begin with first grade, and repeat each grade because the child was homeschooled. Neither have I heard of any issues regarding accepting a previously homeschooled child into a public elementary school. Thus, at the elementary school level, I believe the use of a non-accredited versus an accredited program is a non-issue.

Elementary school is a great time to really enjoy your children while they are little and to explore their excitement over learning together. You can engage in the completion of all kinds of fun elementary school projects and subject-based scavenger hunts. You can go on field trips to museums, zoos, historical sites, and exciting places of business. One of our favorite trips was a tour of the Federal Reserve facility where my boys got to see lots and lots of money and how it is handled by robots on a daily basis. We learned about the Civil War and pioneer life through historical sites and reenactments. We went to the Tennessee Aquarium for their Homeschool Days, and my guys learned a lot by participating in exciting, hands-on experiences at the Aquarium.

For more formalized studies in reading, writing, and history, we used what is known as "narrative nonfiction," which are stories based upon real-life events. There are many great books that children will enjoy when studies are presented as stories rather than dry facts. We utilized Sonlight Curriculum as a source for our narrative nonfiction. We read books and worked on reading skills daily, and we relished our time cuddled up on the couch sharing great books. Some of our best homeschooling days were in the midst of winter, with a fire in the fireplace, hot cocoa to drink, a big blanket to cover everyone on the couch, and a great historical adventure book being read aloud.

For writing at the elementary level, we began with a formal writing curriculum, which rapidly instilled a dislike of writing in my boys. We switched to a program called "Brave Writer," and my guys learned to journal about anything and everything of interest to them. They wrote about our field trips and the stories we were reading, or they created stories of their own. By using journal writing as our primary writing program during elementary school, my guys developed an appreciation for the self-expression they achieved through writing. To me, what is important for a child to learn about writing in elementary school is the basics of how to physically write and to view writing as a form of self-expression and communication.

For math, we used a program that suited my boys' individual learning styles. With one child being a visual learner and the other being a kinesthetic learner, Math-U-See worked well for us with its instructional DVDs and math manipulatives. We supplemented our division instruction with Cuisenaire Rods.

Basically, elementary school should be a fun time spent learning together. Hopefully you can make it fun within the bounds of your state's legal requirements. There are some states that require you to present teaching plans, to select a specific curriculum, and/or to submit to a portfolio review. In those states, you will have to weigh your consideration for "fun" learning with the legal educational requirements in your state. I loved our elementary homeschooling days. Those were our days of building family bonds that will last a lifetime.

Middle School or Junior High

The middle school or junior high school level of education is transitional. The beginning of middle school is often similar to a continuation of elementary school, yet with more robust courses and different instructors for different classes. By the end of middle school, students have often begun taking one or two high school-level classes, and plans are being laid for the students' high school coursework.

With the transitional nature of middle school, if something drastic happened which might necessitate putting a child into public school, such as your death or your spouse's death, timing could play a role in the placement of your child into the public school mid-stream. While it seems far-fetched, we have known a couple of families where tragedy has suddenly struck and a child had to be put into a school so the living or custodial parent could work full-time to support the family. I bring the direness of such a situation up for consideration because it is a possibility, however unlikely, and the consequences will be laid upon your child should you fail to consider the long-term impact of any decision you make.

At the middle school level, accreditation may be beneficial, but it is not by any means necessary. If a child who has been homeschooled has to enter a public middle school during the first year or two of middle school, it is likely there will not be any significant issue with completed coursework or grade placement. If your homeschooled child must be enrolled in a public school during the year before high school, the main issue would be whether or not your child has been working on any high school-level coursework and whether the school will give credit for the coursework completed.

If any specific high school level course is not taken from an accredited source, your local school may or may not give your child credit for that course. If it is a required course and the public school refuses to give course credit, all would not be lost because your child can take the course in high school for credit. Thus, the likely worst-case scenario would be that your public school would refuse to give credit for one or more high school-level courses your child took during middle school and your child would have to take the course again. If a repeat of any class is required, your child would likely make a good grade the second time through the course, which is always good for a student's high school GPA. Although it can be frustrating and disappointing to have to repeat a class, it isn't the end of the world, and over the span of your child's educational career, it won't make any significant difference.

Thus, at the middle school level, the choice about whether to use a formal, accredited type of program has few long-term consequences regardless of whether your child ever needs to enroll in public school or not. There can be benefits for using a regionally accredited source for any high school-level coursework if you want to avoid the possibility of your child having to repeat a course, but it isn't a critical need. Therefore, for middle school, I recommend doing whatever you are comfortable with and enjoying the middle school years as your child matures from an elementary, skills-based learner into a critical-thinker and high school student.

High School

Unlike elementary and middle school, high school coursework is far less likely to be accepted by any regionally accredited high school without rigid proof of completed coursework. Keep in mind that placing a child into high school mid-stream is different from applying to colleges and universities with an unaccredited high school diploma. Many colleges these days will accept unaccredited diplomas from children who have been homeschooled, but not all do, so you will want to investigate the requirements of any college your child may have in mind as a destination.

As far as accreditation goes at the high school level, it can be of significant concern depending upon the circumstances. Having a regionally accredited program is *not required*, but I think any parent is wise to consider the long-term effects of any family tragedy. What if you go under a bus tomorrow? What if your spouse asks for a divorce tomorrow? Would you have to put your children into a traditional school? If not, fabulous! If you're like most of us, there is a possibility that tragic life circumstances would dictate homeschooling is no longer feasible.

At the high school level, the long-term ramifications of using a non-accredited program have been known to cause major headaches and heartaches for a handful of homeschooling families. In our local school system, if a child is not being taught through an accredited program and the child is then enrolled into a public high school, the child does not receive credit for unaccredited coursework done through their homeschool program if they cannot pass a test administered by the school system. Simply put, if the child does not pass a test, he must retake the course from the beginning through the public high school.

Some states, like ours, will test students who seek to enroll in the public school and who want credit for completed coursework. Thus, a child will have to take tests for each completed subject (biology, American history, algebra, world literature, etc.) and the school will grant credit for only those courses for which the child can pass the exam. If your child doesn't test at the needed level of achievement, he would have to repeat the course for credit. If your child does not test well, or if it is later in high school, it could be difficult for your child to recall all he learned in ninth or tenth grade.

We have known families where divorce, cancer, or the death of the primary financial provider forced the families to stop homeschooling. Except in the case where the parents had been using a fully accredited program (accredited by the same accrediting agency that accredits the public high schools), the high school students who were placed into a public school mid-stream had to repeat some of their coursework. Whether it was just a couple of courses (for which exams were not passed) or entire grade levels, the sad fact was that the children suffered further trauma by having some of their prior coursework tossed out the window.

So, as you can probably surmise, accreditation for high school-level coursework requires your serious consideration. Although regional accreditation is not necessary, it may be advisable, particularly if there is any chance your child may need to be enrolled in a public school during her high school career. While parents give up a degree of control over their child's coursework and course choices when going through an accredited program, the oversight, reporting, and involvement of an accrediting body can ease the road of transition when or if changes are needed. Accreditation of your program is not a requirement, but might be desirable.

As a final note for the high school years, if your child works well independently, you may not have any concerns even if something tragic were to happen. There are several online high school programs, GED programs, and other avenues for completing high school which are able to be completed independently by a diligently working student. Although it can be problematic to leave a high school student to fend for herself with her studies, if your student is independent, driven, and able to work hard on her own, she might be able to work independently to finish high school at home even if tragedy strikes a family. If such is the case, an accredited program would be of less importance.

A Little Bit More about Accreditation

If you are going to seek out an accredited program, it is important to know there are many accrediting bodies out there. Some of them are regionally recognized, but many of them are not.

Some of the accrediting bodies that are not typically recognized by public schools, public universities, and colleges are agencies that accredit private schools, religious schools, or distance-education programs. The Accrediting Council for Independent Colleges and Schools, the Distance Education and Training Council, and the Transnational Association of Christian Colleges and Schools are three examples of large accrediting bodies that are not universally accepted for certification of an educational program.

Although a program may be perfectly valid and accredited by one of these agencies, it may not be a program from which a public school is willing to accept certification.

Public schools are accredited by one of the national, regional accrediting agencies. The agencies which accredit public schools, from which public schools will usually accept all valid coursework, are:

- Middle States Association of Colleges and Schools (MSA)
- New England Association of Schools and Colleges (NEASC)
- North Central Association of Colleges and Schools (NCA)
- Northwest Commission on Colleges and Universities (NWCCU)
- Southern Association of Colleges and Schools (SACS)
- Western Association of Schools and Colleges (WASC)

If you are going to seek an accredited program, you might as well use a program certified by one of these regional accrediting agencies; otherwise you may find yourself facing the same or similar issues that you would without any accreditation at all.

Also, having an accredited program can offer a lot of flexibility, depending upon the type of program you use. We used an oversight program that allowed us to select and use whatever curricula or courses we wished, but the program provided oversight for exams, work samples from the student, and tracking of the student's coursework.

There are a couple of programs online that will allow a student to take any accredited course, and the accredited school will accept the courses as part of their program. Most notably, Keystone National High School has traditionally been this type of program. A student must take a minimum number of courses through Keystone, but the student can take other courses from any accredited provider.

The most popular accredited programs are comprehensive high school programs that provide all of the course materials, exams, and instruction through distance education or online coursework. If you don't mind having your child "school at home" rather than truly "homeschooling" (which is picking and choosing whatever you want to use and study at any given time), then using a comprehensive program is an easy—albeit expensive— route. There are several accredited programs that offer a comprehensive high school program that can be completed at home.

Required Subjects

Required subjects can also play a role in educational provisioning should you ever need to cease homeschooling for any reason. As your child advances in his or her schooling, content knowledge becomes increasingly important in order for a child to do well if he is ever re-enrolled in a traditional school.

In this section we consider critical "Standards of Learning," as they are often called by public schools. We also look at resources you can access to determine what your child should know at any grade level.

Elementary

When it comes to elementary school knowledge and skills, I firmly believe that any parent can teach his or her own child. At the elementary level, the basic skills of reading, writing, and math computation are the primary concerns. These skills are the foundational core for success in education as a child gets older. A child with a strong understanding of the basics will be able to learn in higher grades.

Whether a child has an easy time learning these basic skills or demonstrates great difficulty, the one-on-one instruction from a parent who responds to a child's learning needs will eventually lead to educational success. If a child masters the skills easily, the parent's teaching job is easy.

However, if a child has great difficulty learning the core academic skills, a parent may find herself teaching a subject repeatedly and looking for possible solutions to teach the skill by some other means. If a child has difficulty, it is most often still best for the child to be homeschooled where he can get the necessary one-on-one instruction from a loving parent.

If your child is struggling to learn the basics, you may want to join the Learning Abled Kids' Support group at http://groups.yahoo.com/neo/groups/LearningAbledKids/. The group has well over one thousand members homeschooling children who are struggling to learn in one or more areas. The group is designed to help parents find learning solutions for each individual child's learning needs.

Aside from working on the basics, a child can learn a lot about science, history, and social studies through daily life, educational television, educational DVDs, and reading nonfiction or narrative nonfiction that tell the story of factual events. Children also learn about science, history, and social studies quickly and easily through field trips, explorations, museums, history centers, science centers, etc.

An elementary aged child doesn't really need to be drilled in facts, dates, and events on a daily basis in order to learn. In fact, learning from real-life experience is more likely to be retained as permanent experiential learning by a child. Studying facts as workbook lessons often produces only short-term learning that is of little meaningful significance to the individual child. That's not to say that traditional classroom teaching is inadequate, but rather that learning through seeing, hearing, and doing invariably stays with a child best. So, for the elementary years, focus on mastery of the basic skills.

1. Focus on teaching your child how to read everything from the letter sounds, to simple three-letter words, to multi-syllable words, on up to the equivalent of a sixth grade

reading level, and your child will be set to learn anything he needs to learn from books.

2. The required primary skills for writing are learning how to write the letters and words (handwriting), how to form a sentence and paragraphs, and self-expression through writing.

3. For math computation, teach your child counting concepts, time, money skills, addition, subtraction, multiplication, and division, followed by a basic understanding of fractions. If your child masters basic math concepts, has automatic recall of the math facts and gains an understanding of working with fractions by the time he gets to middle school, he will be equipped with the necessary skills for learning higher math concepts.

4. Let science, history, and social studies learning take place naturally. If your child has a passion for dinosaurs, feed his interest with books, DVDs, educational programming, trips to museums, etc. If your child has an interest in World War I, likewise feed his interest. If your child has an interest in art, music, or dance, feed her interest. If your child has an interest in a specific sport, help him learn about and engage in that sports activity. Whatever your child's interests are in elementary school, whether they change frequently or are long-term interests, pursuing your child's interests at his point of curiosity takes advantage of teachable moments where your child is most likely to retain most of what he has learned.

That's it! Make elementary school easy on yourself and your child. The fundamentals are critical for success in the upper grades. Focus on them throughout your child's elementary years and you will have few educational concerns as your child advances in grade levels. Most of all, enjoy the elementary years with your child. The years are fleeting and will be behind you before you know it.

Middle School or Junior High

In middle school, essential knowledge transitions from learning basic academic skills and content knowledge to focusing on reasoning and building a stronger base of foundational knowledge. For the basic skills of reading, writing, and math computation, the middle school years bring a change from learning the skills themselves to learning how these skills can be applied to exploring and communicating understanding of content knowledge.

Science, history, social studies and math reasoning become more prominent as subjects taught. The middle school years seek to establish a stronger understanding of core content knowledge in subjects such as botany, the human body, animal life, the physical sciences, understanding of the history of the United States, the history of the world, history of ancient peoples, as well as an introduction of more advanced math reasoning through the manipulation of core math computations.

Core skill mastery in reading, writing, and mathematical computation should be strongly established by the time a child reaches sixth grade. If a child is still struggling to learn any of these core skills when entering sixth grade, a strong remedial focus should occur throughout middle school. A child without a firm foundation in reading, writing, and math is very likely to struggle with learning in high school.

Thus, if your child has been in another school environment and has not been given a solid foundation in the core academic skills, there is a high likelihood that continued teaching in the same educational placement is not going to bring about a meaningful change. Changing to homeschooling, a private tutoring program, or some other avenue should be explored.

If your child has been homeschooled to this point and is still having difficulty grasping core skills, it is time to seek additional help in identifying the causes of your child's learning struggles. While middle school isn't too late to begin remedial programs, it is ideal if all remediation can be completed before high school.

Many parents want to ignore problems: They hope their child will outgrow them, or they assume their child is lazy or unmotivated. Believe me, no child WANTS to be unable to read, unable to write, or unable to perform basic calculations. If your child's attitude has become one of total disinterest, it is likely because he has come to believe he can't learn these skills. It's best to seek help now, before the high school years. Thus, in particular, if your child is behind, meeting his needs with new passion and diligence is essential in middle school.

If your child mastered the core academic skills easily while in elementary school, middle school can easily become a "break away" period—a time to move ahead of most middle schoolers and into the initial high school-level studies. If a child is ready to learn specific subjects such as biology, world history, literature, etc. on a deeper level, there is no reason to hold her back. Beginning high school-level coursework in seventh or eighth grade will permit a student to begin college-level work toward the end of high school, which can be very helpful for any child who wants to attend college. Even if your child doesn't know if he wants to eventually go to college, advancing studies as he is able works well.

In middle school, it is typical for a parent to wonder what topics their child should study in sixth, seventh or eighth grade. A great free resource for this kind of information is any state's published standards for their own school programs. Most states publish some type of "Standards of Learning," "Core Academic Competencies," "Essential Knowledge Standards," or some aptly named documentation regarding what children are expected to learn at any given level of their education. If you search for your state's Department of Education website and look for curriculum information, you can probably find the expected core knowledge standards there. In fact, you can look for any state's core knowledge standards and follow those as there is no ultimate right or wrong set of standards.

Truthfully, unless your state laws require it, you don't really even need to follow standards. Any published textbook or basic curriculum is going to include a well-developed exploration of topics that are beneficial to study as a foundation for high school. The published standards are free and easily accessed, though, if you want to use narrative nonfiction, projects, or other forms of educating your child that do not directly involve the use of a published textbook or curriculum.

At the middle school level, you can still use foundational science, history, and social studies books in the form of the narrative nonfiction approach for meaningful, real-life, relational understanding of concepts. Project-based and experiential learning is still an excellent choice that can help keep boredom with schoolwork from setting in.

With all that said, middle school is still primarily foundational in nature when it comes to academic study. As such, it's unlikely you would need to seek classes or instruction outside of your own provisioning within your homeschool with the possible exception of remedial or very advanced learners. In either of those cases, having outside assistance can be helpful, but how to proceed with your specific learner's needs is outside the scope of this particular book. If your child needs remedial help, look for my upcoming book Overcoming Learning Disabilities as a great guide for how to meet the needs of any child who is struggling with learning the core academic skills.

High School

High school is an entirely different educational world than either elementary or middle school. When a child enters high school, unless the child knows precisely what he wants to do or be when he finishes school, one must provide an educational path that will stand with any career or college path your child might choose. Even if your child thinks he knows exactly what vocation he wants to pursue when he is an adult, his ideas can, and often do, change over time. Thus, I recommend approaching high school with the highest level of educational need in mind. Therefore it is advisable to approach high school with the assumption that your child will want to go to college.

Do not think assuming your child will want to go to college means every class must be advanced placement, honors, or at an advanced level for college preparation, or that any class must be advanced. Your child does not have to take a single advanced placement or honors class in high school. He can still be prepared to attend college with ordinary high school classes.

Approaching high school as if your child will eventually desire to go to college does mean you should approach the high school coursework with an eye on meeting the basic admission requirements of most colleges. The majority of high schools have similar requirements, and generally speaking, you would be safe assuming your child will get into some college somewhere if he is academically competent and takes the following courses during high school:

• <u>Four English Courses</u> - two composition courses, two literature courses   (American Lit. and World Lit.)

• <u>Four Math Courses</u> - Algebra 1, Algebra 2, geometry, a higher math (pre-calculus, statistics, trigonometry, etc.)

- <u>Four Science Courses</u> – biology, chemistry, physics, one "elective" science (anatomy, oceanography, botany, etc.)

- <u>Four History Courses</u> – U.S. history, world history, American government, economics.

- <u>Foreign Language</u> – levels 1 & 2 of the same language.

- One <u>PE Course</u>
- One <u>Health Course</u>
- One <u>Art, Music, Dance, or Drama Course</u>
- One <u>Computer or Technology Course</u>
- Two or more <u>Electives</u>

To fulfill this coursework, each year of high school will consist of six classes (maybe seven if your child wishes to take more electives). Each year your child would take:

1. English class
2. Math class
3. Science class
4. Social Studies class
5. PE, Health, Technology OR Arts class
6. Foreign Language or an elective
7. An additional elective can be added in any year if your child wishes to take an additional course, but it isn't necessary.

Following these guidelines will, generally speaking, provide an appropriate course of study for most colleges. If your child has an idea about which college he or she may want to attend, it would be a wise move to visit the college's admissions page and learn about their specific high school course of study requirements. I don't currently know of any college which would not consider the listed courses as a viable college preparatory course of study, but that could change with time, so don't hesitate to check with several colleges to be sure the listed courses would fulfill the needed entrance requirements.

Using the academic plan I have provided, you can seek out courses in each subject area from any number of curriculum providers, textbook publishers, online classes, or classes taught online or locally through a community college as joint enrollment courses (usually after tenth grade has been completed). The courses can be as advanced or as common as you'd like. When it comes to your child's high school transcript, for college admission purposes, it is the course of study that is most important. Colleges with highly competitive admissions want to see advanced coursework on high school transcripts, so you will need to consider an advanced course of study if your child is likely to apply to universities with highly competitive admissions.

Should you select the simplest or most difficult courses you can possibly find? If your child wants to go to college, the more challenging the studies, the better prepared your child will be for college and the more likely he will be to succeed. Thus, it is usually wise to choose a challenging level of coursework you know your child is capable of completing which will also require your student to put forth meaningful effort in order to be successful.

For some students, it will take highly advanced coursework to provide a meaningful level of challenge. For other students, ordinary, mass-published textbooks and courses for "average" students will provide plenty of challenge. I do not say this to diminish, by any means, the level of achievement of any child who is completing a high school course of study, but rather to make clear the level of challenge presented by trying to complete coursework that is too advanced for any given student can sometimes be more detrimental than beneficial. It is usually beneficial and best to work at a threshold which will not cause too much unnecessary stress for your high school student and which will provide a reasonable likelihood the student will succeed when practicing diligence with his studies.

As an additional help for high school, there are programs available that will help you track your child's studies and help you create a professional-looking transcript. Check out former homeschooling mom, Lee Binz's Total Transcript Solution program as a great help for tracking your student's coursework and creating an up–to-date transcript when your child applies for college or a job.

While high school can seem the scariest as far as homeschooling goes, it really is the easiest when you can find good classes or programs, and if your child is able to learn independently. During high school, my guys have been mostly self-taught with guidance from me or my husband and, in those cases where they took outside classes, with help from their instructors.

For the duration of high school, my job has primarily been administrative in nature. My job has been to plan the boys' coursework, find appropriate courses or curricula, grade their schoolwork (in the case of at-home classes), and track their studies using the spreadsheets I have created for those purposes. My boys' independent studying, learning, and completing the actual assignments proved to be great preparation for college because they have learned independent planning and class management skills that are invaluable for college students.

That said, don't let high school scare you! We reassessed our homeschooling at the end of middle school, and I was afraid to go forward into the high school years. My fear stemmed from uncertainty and a sense of ultimate responsibility if we failed to do the job right. Luckily, we received direction from several sources and have found ourselves at the end of a stellar and successful high school path.

Late Starts

If you are just beginning to homeschool in middle or high school because your child is behind academically, or because it has become evident that public school is not going to meet your child's educational or psychological needs, let me talk briefly to you about special considerations under these circumstances.

There are many parents who keep hoping things will turn around or improve academically or socially for their child throughout elementary school. By middle school, a creepy feeling crawls into their minds telling them, "Things are only going to get worse from here." If your child is academically more than one year behind peers, chances are high that things will not get better if your child remains in the same school system. Thus, homeschooling can become a means for rescuing your child from academic failure or severe depression caused by any number of social issues at school. Rather than risking your child failing to graduate, dropping out, or worse, you are wise to consider an alternative path for the completion of high school.

Far Behind, Entering Middle School

If you're starting to homeschool in middle school and your child is far behind, you shouldn't have too difficult of a time. Your child is likely young enough that you can still mend his self-beliefs about his ability to learn and his worthiness as an individual person. You have time to bring about educational successes without too much stress. Your homeschooling efforts will require diligence and a high degree of attentiveness to your child's needs, but you can do it!

Facing the prospect of our older son going into middle school unable to read was the eye-opening, pivotal moment for my husband and me. Thankfully, it was not too late for our rescue efforts. From both an academic and self-esteem standpoint my husband and I felt we were on a rescue mission to save our son. He needed rescuing both academically and from depression.

Let me say to you, the middle school years are precious. They are the perfect time to talk with your child about his heart-felt feelings about himself, his academic abilities, his interests, his dreams, and how he envisions his life ahead. Your child is cognitively old enough to talk with as if he is an adult, and I recommend you talk to your child deeply on an earnest level. Ask him about his feelings, hopes, desires, and dreams. These can help you lay out a blueprint for homeschooling which will help your child realize the outcome he desires. After all, finishing out high school toward a trade, career, or college is based upon what your child needs and wants in life, to help your child become a fulfilled person.

Although my son expressed a desire NOT to homeschool, he also said he wanted to go to college and become a scientist in some field. Given that he could not yet read, we made an agreement with him that we would work with him throughout middle school to teach him to read, and he could return to public school when he could read well enough to be successful in regular high school classes. We made our agreement with each other and set upon our path of overcoming the learning difficulties my son faced throughout elementary school. We were highly successful. In fact, we were so successful, by the time my son reached ninth grade he could read at a 13+ grade equivalent. He also loved homeschooling so much, he no longer had any interest whatsoever in returning to public school, so we plowed full-steam ahead into high school and beyond.

By the time my son graduated from high school, he had 39 credit hours of college coursework behind him, so he went to his chosen university as a college sophomore. As I had always suspected, my son was quite capable of learning—and learning well—regardless of what the public school administrators and teachers told us.

I hope our story is an inspiration as you head into middle school with your child. Beginning to homeschool in middle school affords you a bit of time to play catch-up before your child begins high school. If your child is in eighth grade and about to enter high school, you'll want to give consideration to the next section as well because the grace period for remediation you have available is somewhat shortened.

Far Behind, Entering High School

If you're starting to homeschool in high school and your child is far behind, you have your work cut out for you. Right from the beginning, I think it is helpful to reframe your mindset about what is acceptable in terms of preparing for life after high school and graduation dates. If a child is capable of performing schoolwork on only a sixth grade level, he is not prepared for college even if he is chronologically old enough to graduate from high school at the end of this school year. I've actually had a parent want to know how to get her son, under similar criteria, into college. My suggestion: Take a year or two to work diligently on his core academic skills and then consider college readiness.

My point is this: No matter how behind your child may be at this moment, do not despair or fret. There is no required timeframe that dictates your child must graduate from high school when he is eighteen and dive right into college, training or a career. Yes, that is the typical scenario for most teens, but when given atypical circumstances or learning, there is absolutely nothing that says you must start college at the same time as everyone else. It is better to take a gap year (or two) and refine those core academic skills than it is to jump right into college with a student who is not prepared because he may then go down an avenue of failure.

Trust me—I began college when I was twenty-three. Most of my classmates were younger and more immature than I, which enhanced my ability to do well in my classes.

So, if your child is starting high school and is behind, what should you do? First of all, if you don't already have a comprehensive understanding of your child's learning challenges, learning strengths, learning needs, and learning style, you must obtain this information. If your child's educational needs have not been met by any instructional method that has been applied to his learning to this point, doing more of the same type of instruction is not going to suddenly equal effective learning. You must obtain a deep understanding of your child's learning needs and then seek to meet them.

If your child hasn't had a recent comprehensive neuro-psychological or psycho-educational evaluation, or never had one at all, your child will be best served by obtaining an evaluation as soon as possible. This would not be the type of simplistic evaluation often provided by schools, but an in-depth assessment of your child's academic aptitude, information processing, attention functioning, comprehension and reasoning skills, etc. A comprehensive evaluation looks at all of the cognitive processes that may interfere with learning. A high quality provider will also offer recommendations about how to overcome or work around any cognitive deficits that exist.

A comprehensive evaluation enables you to move past the generalized determination that your child is "behind in reading" by determining the root cause of reading difficulties. If you know the root cause, you can work with programs that help overcome the specific roadblock rather than trying any number of solutions that don't meet your child's specific needs.

When or if you have a comprehensive evaluation, go through it with a fine-toothed comb—twice. First, read through the report and write down notes for every area where your child has a "relative strength," performs above average or in the superior range, and where your child shows no difficulty. Whether your child's advanced skills are in oral reading fluency, verbal comprehension, visual-motor integration, or any of a wide number of other assessed areas, you should make note of every cognitive process that is a strength for your child. These are the avenues through which your child will learn most effectively. If you can match your instruction with your child's strengths, your child will get far more out of the instruction than if it does not match his needs.

The second time you read through the comprehensive evaluation with a fine-toothed comb, make notes for areas of "relative weakness," where your child performs below average or in the deficient range, and where your child shows notable difficulty. You will want to avoid teaching through weak avenues of cognition and find ways to overcome weaknesses by coming at them through strengths.

For example, if your child has difficulty with mathematical reasoning and reading comprehension, he probably has difficulty figuring out math problems presented as word problems. He may have decent skills in mathematical computation (he knows his math facts), and he may be able to solve numerical problems such as $49 + 51$. Your child may also have a relative strength in visual-motor integration, the grooved peg-board test, or other motor skills. In such a case, it is probably more effective to use visuals and manipulatives to teach mathematical reasoning concepts than it is to have your child continue to use a typical math textbook where learning is based upon reading comprehension. Looking for a math curriculum that uses visuals and manipulatives and then following that curriculum will likely bring about better math-learning outcomes than continuing with traditional math textbooks, pencil, and paper.

It takes creativity and thinking outside of the box to find

learning solutions that utilize your child's learning strengths and avoid his weaknesses, but the payoff can be huge. The key is to understand that whatever has been typically used from elementary school until high school has obviously not been very effective if your child is behind. Thus, you must seek to provide education differently in order to get better results. "Differently" can be as simple as bringing a child home to work one-on-one if a child is easily distracted in a regular classroom. If a child has a slow processing speed and needs more time to assimilate information he is presented, simply coming home to allow ample thinking time before the next piece of information is presented can help.

Your primary goal for helping your child is not to complete high school on time, but to complete it well. If you can spend some amount of time deeply focused on improving reading, writing, and/or math skills (whatever is needed), you can work on the high school subjects through accommodations at the same time.

For a child who has difficulty with reading, you can use audiobook editions of textbooks or use DVD-based, lecture-style curriculum. For a child who has difficulty with writing, you can become his scribe or use dictation software such as Dragon Naturally Speaking to allow your child to use oral dictation to get his ideas onto paper. And for math computation, your child can use a calculator while you work on math facts. These are all standard accommodations which can enable your child to continue with grade-level studies while you work on remediation of needed skills.

The bottom line is that if your child is entering high school and is academically far behind, as long as he is capable of learning, your child can complete a high school-level course of study with tools of accommodation, lots of support from you, and hard work on both of your parts. If you want to ensure your child graduates from high school adequately prepared for his chosen vocation or career, you must put in the time, energy, and work to ensure your child gets what he needs educationally in order to be successful in life. The point of high school is to make sure your child is actually prepared for adult life, and the most important academic skills for any adult are the core skills of reading, writing, and doing math.

Completing a certain course of study is required for college admission and some technical schools, so it is best if your child does follow a formal course of study in addition to acquiring the core skills. That said, you can use the information about high school requirements in the earlier chapter to plan which courses your child should complete. Do not worry if your courses are not based upon traditional textbooks because your goal is for your child to learn the content and concepts, and learning can take place through many channels, some of which may be the History Channel, Discovery Channel, National Geographic, etc.

As an example, we bought the History Channel's Classroom DVD series on US history to use for our US history learning. By watching every DVD and answering questions about what they learned, my boys learned a lot about US history, why things happened, how they happened, as well as where and when they happened. They learned more than they would have had I handed them a standard textbook for their US history courses.

In this regard, history and science are the easiest to teach through audio-visual content, but literature can be taught this way too using movies based upon classics such as Hamlet, Romeo and Juliet, Huckleberry Finn, etc. Math is probably the most challenging to teach outside of a textbook, but there are options available for audio-visual teaching there too. Many parents like to use Teaching Textbooks or Math-U-See with its DVDs. Search and ye shall find!

There are options for completing high school that don't require your child to be able to read or write at this moment. Math does require an understanding of how to work with the math facts before one can work with equations, but using a different style of curriculum may be your key to success.

5 LIFESTYLE TRANSFORMATION

I love living the homeschooling lifestyle! Becoming a homeschooling family can transform your daily lives in ways you may not have anticipated. Before we began homeschooling, I had no clue the types of changes we would see within our family and in our lifestyle. There are many positive changes—and an economic change that is a bit more challenging. I'll address the economic challenges in the next section, but first I wanted to share some of the sometimes surprising changes we experienced when shifting from public school to homeschooling.

Reconnecting As a Family

When your kids go to public school, your days are often harried and stressful during the week. Your kids get up in the morning, get ready for school, and rush out the door, and if you're lucky, you can have a brief conversation as they're getting ready. In our experience, when our boys were in public school, mornings were usually rushed as I made lunches and my boys got ready for school so we seldom had time for meaningful morning conversation.

Once we began homeschooling, we were able to have leisurely mornings, slowly waking up, and calmly getting dressed and ready for our day. When you homeschool, you can take your time and have a relaxed, fulfilling breakfast with lots of connected conversation with your child. When you start your day at a natural pace, everybody is much more relaxed, and this sets the stage for a better day of learning. It also gives you the opportunity to talk with your child on a daily basis about his concerns, struggles with learning, dreams, hopes, and plans for the day. This allows you to really know and understand the heart of your child. Connecting in this way helps to build strong bonds of family relationships that can withstand all sorts of trials and tribulations that may come along the path of life.

When you're homeschooling, you can connect with your child throughout the day. You know precisely which subjects are giving him difficulty, which subjects he is passionate about, which subjects he is apathetic about, and exactly what kind of school day he has had without having to ask.

If your child is in public school, he has a day in which you are not a participant at all. If you're lucky, at the end of the school day, you will have the opportunity to connect with your child about his school day. However, as is often the case when a child is in public school, his day continues to be stressful after school as he tries to complete assigned homework, participates in activities he's involved in, and tries to complete other required responsibilities. Sometimes a child is exhausted when he gets home from school and has no interest in recapping his day for an inquiring parent. Most families I know have little time to connect with their children in a meaningful way at the end of the school day, thus over time the family relationships becomes more distanced and more disconnected.

When homeschooling, at the end of the day, all of your schoolwork is done because there is no homework, and often activities take place during the day, which leaves the evenings open for family time or time with friends. The benefit of this time spent with each other, connecting on a daily basis, cannot be underestimated. Over time it allows you to truly know the heart and spirit of your child. When you know all of your child's hopes and dreams, struggles and demons, you can help your child fulfill the first two and guide him in dealing with the last two. Your guidance and input into your child's life helps everyone in the family as your support builds relationship bonds that can scarcely be broken.

As a parent you get to be the primary influence in your child's personal development rather than having peers and teachers at school as the primary inputs for your child's guidance. Depending upon your child's status in school, peer input, teacher input, and guidance from others can be either positive or extremely negative. In particular, if your child is bullied, the input to his spirit is undoubtedly negative. Over time, this type of daily hammering can cause lasting damage to your child's self-esteem and ability to do well in school. If your homeschool provides a peaceful and supportive environment, your child's self-esteem can grow strong, and his learning achievement can surpass any measure of achievement he might accomplish in public school.

Needless to say, having an uplifting and supportive environment where you can connect with your children will build family ties that are stronger than those you can build with your child going away to school each day. As your children grow up and become teens, you could quite possibly see substantial differences between the relationship you have with your child versus the relationships parents have with their children who go to public school. I know many homeschooled teens who love and respect their parents in ways that seems foreign to their peers in public school where the mindset of teens is often one of defiance toward parents or authority figures.

Homeschooling can transform your family relationships if you build a calm, peaceful, loving home; every minute you spend together will be more precious than the most brilliant diamond. As far as the benefits of homeschooling goes, this is among the most unexpected and most valuable.

Vacations as Learning Opportunities

One of my favorite things about homeschooling is our ability to take family vacations whenever we want. This was a surprising benefit of homeschooling. Because we are no longer constrained to the school calendar, we can take our vacations during the off-season, which saves us money and often allows us to use facilities when there are no crowds to contend with.

As an example, early in our homeschooling years we took a family vacation to Disney World in February. The timing was perfect. There were no lines for any of the attractions, and we got deep discounts, had no problem with reservations, and had most of the park to ourselves. Throughout our homeschooling years we have always taken our vacations during periods of time when public school is in session. This allows us to experience attractions at a more leisurely and meaningful pace.

You can also use your family vacations as learning opportunities. Whenever we traveled to a destination, we often sought out historical sites, museums, science centers, and other educationally oriented attractions. If you go off-season, the staff are often more available and willing to spend extra time teaching and explaining the features of the attraction, its historical significance, or the meaning behind displays to your children. This makes the visits much more productive from a learning standpoint than they are when there are lots of people.

Given that you can travel whenever you choose, you can also take schoolwork with you and engage in schooling while traveling. So even if your family is on a vacation, that doesn't mean all schooling stops. In reality it allows you and your family to live a learning lifestyle. Your children can learn about history, the people of any geographic region you travel to, and the culture, the art, and the historical significance of important sites. Every vacation can become a unit study, which will be more meaningful and remain with your children longer because they have actually experienced the area they are learning about rather than reading about it in a book.

For example, prior to going on a vacation to Orlando, where they have the Animal Kingdom, Epcot, Disney World, and SeaWorld nearby, I made folders for each of our boys with information pages about many of the odd animals I knew they would see during our visit, the countries that are represented in Epcot Center, and some of the books represented by the rides at Disney World, like the Swiss Family Robinson, Snow White, Cinderella, etc.

Before we left, we didn't tell our boys where we were going. Instead, we departed early in the morning, and when they began asking where we were going, we had them read their notebooks and guess where we were going. We were about four hours into our trip when they figured it out in its entirety. (They were initially confused by the animals and countries included in their books.) After they figured out where we were going, we gave them each a map with our route highlighted and taught them how to follow where we were physically with the map location. That was among our best planned homeschool vacations that incorporated a lot of learning and pre-planning.

When Dad or Mom has to travel on business, the whole family can sometimes travel to the business destination. The family can spend time together in the evening, outside of business hours, and experience the dining and city lights of the region. During the daytime, the homeschooling parent and children can visit museums, national or state parks, or other sites nearby while the working parent is in meetings, training, or otherwise occupied with business.

While this isn't always possible if the business travel is via air travel, it is frequently an option for any trip that can be undertaken by automobile. If the business trip is long enough and the driving distance to the destination is manageable, the family can often travel by car and arrive after the business traveler has arrived by airplane. For some destinations that offer countless educational opportunities, you may find a combined education-business trip may be ideal. Washington DC is just such a destination where you can tour many government buildings and the Smithsonian. Given the opportunity to travel there under any circumstance, a homeschooling family would find the experience to be educational in countless ways.

Additionally, homeschooling allows your family to travel and visit with friends and family at any time, which can be of great benefit in establishing the heritage of your family. We found that being able to visit distant relatives, to learn about our family history and different lifestyles, has enriched our children's lives and built stronger family bonds with our extended family. Being able to travel at any time also allows you to provide support during family crises, medical emergencies, and to support elderly family members in their time of need. Connecting with family and providing support in this way helps establish family roots for your child's lifetime.

Being able to travel and take family vacations whenever we want is just one of the great surprises we found when we began homeschooling. Living our lives at a more leisurely pace, traveling when family beckons, and traveling during off-seasons have made times of travel much more fulfilling and relaxing because we are not restricted to traveling based upon a school's calendar. It all adds up to a more natural flow to our family life.

Fun with Field Trips

While in public school, field trip days can be among the most exciting days of the school year. Unfortunately, there are seldom more than one or two field trips per school year because of the logistics of taking a large group of children on a field trip. As a homeschooling family, you can go on a trip with your immediate family only, plan to meet up with a friend or two, or visit locations on specified "Homeschool" days.

For example, Stone Mountain Park has a designated Homeschool Day each fall, and homeschooling families throughout Georgia and in the Southeast take advantage of the discounts and activities in order to participate in a field trip to Stone Mountain.

When you are homeschooling, field trip days are every bit as exciting as typical school days. The great thing about homeschooling field trips is your ability to plan and take an outing on any day in any subject. We had a group of friends who created a "Middle School History" field trip group. Once a month we would pack our picnic lunches and head for a venue to meet with our homeschool friends. On some of our historical field trips, we visited the Georgia Mountain Center, Chickamauga Battle Field, Kennesaw Mountain Battlefield, the National Civil War Naval Museum, Atlanta History Museum, Stone Mountain, and other locations of interest. Meeting with other homeschool families, even if it is only one or two other families, can add an element of excitement and fun to the outing.

As you are laying out your educational plans for the month or year, you can consider field trip opportunities in each subject. That one year we focused on history field trips, but every other year we planned a wide variety of field trips that allowed us to explore many different subjects. Our field trips included the High Museum of Art, the Federal Reserve Bank, the Atlanta Zoo, the Atlanta Botanical Gardens, the State Botanical Gardens, the Chattanooga Aquarium, the Georgia Aquarium, the Centennial National Park, the Coca-Cola Museum, the Aurora Theater to see a play, the Center for Puppetry Arts, the Atlanta Symphony Orchestra school program, the Fernbank Science Center and Planetarium, and many more.

Most academic years we opted for approximately one field trip per quarter because we had so many activities going on; otherwise we would have had to limit our number of outings to stay focused on our academics. When you are homeschooling, particularly in a large metropolitan area, there are so many choices for destinations, activities, and one-time opportunities that you have to be selective. Otherwise, you can end up overbooking your schedule which can wear you out!

If you are a highly energetic person, you might really enjoy being on the go, experiencing hands-on learning at every opportunity. We know quite a few people who stay on the go. They take books to read, workbooks, and even laptops to complete schoolwork in the car in what is known as "carschooling." There are even books available about how to carschool.

At times we did undertake carschooling, but ours was more along the lines of traditional schooling, or activities that related to our destination as described in the prior section about vacationing. Most often we took workbooks or books to read in the car with us as we headed to and from scheduled activities, outings, and on vacations.

The homeschooling lifestyle becomes a way of living and learning throughout your days in various ways. Traditional learning tools (books, audiobooks, workbooks, and even DVDs these days) can be taken on the road to wherever your day's destination may be. You are no longer limited in the number of sites you can visit with your child because of your child being in school. You are free to visit any venue any time of any day and are limited only by your own personal scheduling and financial means. The lifestyle of learning is very freeing and provides for many memorable moments that last a lifetime.

Education outside the Box

While we are talking about learning vacations, homeschool field trips, and carschooling, it's a good time to talk about learning outside the lines. What is learning? In its simplest sense, learning is the acquisition of knowledge and understanding. Are books required for learning? No. Are pencils, pens, notebooks, and lectures required for learning? No. Learning can take place through first-person experiences, hands-on activities, seeing, hearing, and doing.

Traditional schools must manage a large number of learners who are easier to manage and control if they are sitting at a desk with a book, reading, or listening to a teacher. The practicality of working with a large number of students using books and lectures works reasonably well when working with masses of children, but teaching and learning in this format is not always effective. If a child has a visual learning style or is a hands-on, kinesthetic learner, particularly when a non-traditional learning style is coupled with learning challenges, then the child may not learn well at all from traditional teaching. Thus, teaching outside the box can often bring about greater learning benefits for any child who does not learn well inside the traditional school box.

Learning Style-Based Learning

There are several different learning styles models used to assess a child's learning preferences. The primary learning styles models are VAKT (Visual, Auditory, Kinesthetic/Tactile), Gardner's Multiple Intelligences, and the Dunn and Dunn Model for Learning Domains. Undertaking a process of analyzing your child to determine his or her individual learning needs through each of these models will help you provide instruction in a way that is most helpful to your learner. Providing instruction that is not within your child's preferred learning style can waste your time and effort and frustrate your learner because she will not be able to easily gain needed knowledge from the instruction you provide.

As a homeschooling family, you are better able to tailor instruction to your individual child than any teacher can in a traditional classroom environment. A traditional classroom teacher simply does not have the planning time, resources, or ability to assess the individual learning preferences of each child in her classroom and then provide individualized instruction that meets the individual child's needs. It simply isn't going to happen unless that teacher is a miracle worker! This is where you are blessed to be able to homeschool because you can meet your child's individual learning needs to whatever extent you decide to pursue.

Given that you want to teach outside the box and teach your child in the most effective way possible, let's explore each of the three learning style models previously listed.

The VAKT learning styles model is probably the most widely used and understood way of separating individual learning preferences. Let's look at each of the styles more closely:

- VISUAL: When a learner takes in information through his eyes, he processes the information in the visual, picture-oriented center of his brain. Most aptly shared by Temple Grandin in her book, Thinking in Pictures, Expanded Edition: My Life with Autism, her way of thinking is entirely visual. For learners whose strength is in processing visual images, typical teaching through talking, reading, or language-based learning will not bring the highest level of learning progress. However, if teaching is provided through rich imagery, charts, graphs, and other visual depictions of information, then your visual learner will process the information with the greatest efficiency using his visual processing strengths. Documentary films, picture-rich books, hands-on demonstrations, and means of teaching that allow a visual learner to watch or process images are among the most effective ways of teaching a visual learner. Keep in mind that reading itself is language based and is therefore primarily processed in the auditory center of the brain. I do not classify reading as a "visual" activity because the visual involvement is limited to processing the letter symbol in order to find a sound correlation for the purpose of forming words (language).

• AUDITORY: When a learner takes in information through his ears, through lecture or through reading, the information is language based in nature because the information must be processed in the language center of the brain. The vast majority of traditional teaching is taught toward an auditory learning style, so if a child has an auditory learning style, he is most likely to be successful in a traditional classroom. When teaching a child with an auditory learning style, any teacher has a greater ability to find ready-made curricula that meet the needs of an auditory learner. If your child is an auditory learner, you don't have to be as concerned with thinking outside of the traditional school box when looking for ways to effectively teach your child.

• KINESTHETIC/TACTILE: The least common and the most problematic in a traditional classroom is the kinesthetic/tactile learning style. Learners who learn best by actively doing things and through hands-on activities and bodily movement are active learners who require modifications of most instructional materials in order to best meet their individual needs. In traditional classrooms, these are the learners who are most likely to be fidgety, in and out of their desks, swinging their legs, and are otherwise unable to "sit still" at the request of their teacher. When a child has a kinesthetic/tactile learning style, if he is not moving, he is not learning as effectively as he would be if he were moving. Thus, if you are homeschooling an active learner, he will probably learn best if you let him bounce on a big exercise ball while reading, jump on a mini-trampoline while working on flash cards, or rock in a rocking chair while looking at books. Even better would be to move toward project-based or experiential learning where your child can build, make, act, and otherwise experience everything he is learning.

While these are considered the most well known of the learning styles, the truth is that each person learns through all of the learning styles to varying degrees. A person may have a preference for visuals or hands-on activities, but she will still learn some content through hearing the information.

For the most effective means of teaching and reinforcement, it is smart to assess your child for his primary learning style then obtain instructional materials that utilize that means of teaching most heavily. Reinforcement of the information through the other learning styles will help the child remember the information better. Using all three styles in teaching activities is called multisensory instruction, which has been shown to be the most effective means of providing instruction overall.

As an instructional example, let's assume your child is primarily a visual learner and you want to teach him about volcanoes. By planning instructional activities in each mode of learning, you will give your child a rich learning experience. You might begin by watching the National Geographic Volcano! DVD, then read a picture-rich book such as The Best Book of Volcanoes, then follow the learning DVD and book with building a volcano model. Using three different means for providing the instruction, with visual learning elements accompanying the auditory and K/T activities, will enable your child to remember a larger portion of the information presented and to understand volcanoes. You can learn more about the VAKT Learning

Styles at: http://learningabledkids.com/learning-styles/vakt-visual-auditory-kinesthetic-tactile/.

Gardner's Multiple Intelligences is another widely known model for determining a child's learning style. I like to think of Gardner's model as a way of looking at a child's natural inclinations and talents, which may be used to enhance learning. The nine styles Gardner has identified are:

- Logical-mathematical
- Spatial
- Linguistic
- Bodily-kinesthetic
- Musical
- Existential
- Inter-personal
- Intra-personal
- Naturalistic

Most of the intelligence types are relatively self-explanatory when you consider the titles. When you are teaching your child, you can utilize his area of personal intelligence as a means for approaching teaching. For example, if your child is musical, you might find that memorizing facts by using jingles, songs, or poems might help your child remember the content more easily. If a child is inter-personal in nature, then engaging in group activities with other children or question and answer sessions with you can help with learning.

By helping your child understand his own personal intelligence and teaching him to use it for his own benefit in learning and life, you can give your child a sense of confidence and pride in his own unique areas of ability. You can even have your child think of musical, social, or other ways of learning his lessons to give him a sense of ownership of his own intelligence.

Perhaps one of my favorite learning styles models is the Dunn and Dunn Learning Style Model (D&D Model). The D&D Model is more focused on a child's environmental, psychological, social, physiological, and emotional needs than it is specifically on how a child learns. When trying to establish the best learning environment for your child, considering each of the domains in the D&D Model can be very helpful for minimizing factors that interfere with your child's learning. The D&D Model considers five functional domains that affect the learning readiness of a child in any given situation. Let's look briefly at each of the domains:

1. Environmental
   A. Sound
   B. Light
   C. Temperature
   D. Seating

2. Emotional
   A. Motivation
   B. Responsibility/Conformity
   C. Task Persistence
   D. Structure

3. Sociological
   A. Self
   B. Pair
   C. Peers
   D. Team
   E. Adult
   F. Variety

4. Physiological
   A. Perceptual
   B. Intake
   C. Time of Day
   D. Mobility

5. Psychological
   A. Analytic / Global
   B. Reflective / Impulsive

As far as assessment tools go, the preferences in the D&D Model can be determined best through their online learning styles inventory found at:
http://www.learningstyles.net/en/our-assessments.

Using this learning styles inventory, you can establish a learning environment and learning routines that meet your child's individual needs. If your child likes a quiet, softly lit, cozy location for studying, you can create that space. If your child likes a bright, sunny room with a table and chairs, you can create a space that will meet his study needs. While the D&D Model itself doesn't address the way a child learns as much as it addresses the development of an optimal environment for your child's availability to learning, it is a valuable model that enables you to establish the best possible learning environment for your child.

By combining these three models with your own knowledge of your child, you can find ways to enhance learning through an individualized program tailored to your child's needs. While critics complain about a child needing to learn to fit into the real world and individualized instruction at this level is a disservice to the child, if your child is struggling with learning in a typical classroom environment, it makes little sense to waste the child's time sitting in an ineffective learning environment. If a child cannot cope with the bright lights, noise, and distractions of a typical classroom, he may not learn much about anything. Does it really make sense to send the child to an ineffective learning environment every day when the primary goal is learning?

One has to consider the purpose of going to school. It is to learn. If your child isn't learning because he is being bullied, distracted, disinterested, or depressed about school, then the child is not going to benefit from his educational provisioning. Given you want your child to progress educationally, setting up a viable learning environment for your child can help your child be more academically engaged. If he progresses academically and has his social needs met, there are plenty of opportunities otherwise in life for a mature adult to learn how to "fit in" to the real world.

One other thought: Critics sometimes believe that homeschooling makes a child socially awkward. I ask you, are there socially awkward children who aren't homeschooled? Of course there are. Those children are the most likely to be bullied, to not fit in, and to otherwise have difficulty coping in a standard classroom. Their parents are more likely to witness social, learning, and emotional problems with their child in a traditional school and may choose to homeschool the child. The child would not be socially awkward because she is homeschooled, but rather she would be homeschooled because she is socially awkward.

Conversely, are there highly social, typical children who are homeschooled? Of course there are, and many of them! People homeschool for a wide variety of reasons and homeschooling itself does not change the personality or social adeptness of a child. A child's personality, sociability, and academic aptitude are not caused by homeschooling. A child's personality is what it is, whether the child is at a traditional school or homeschooled. Some children learn more when in a group-oriented, social setting. Some children learn better when taught one-to-one. No matter what your child's needs are, homeschooling will not make your child socially awkward unless you purposefully isolate him from all other people. Neither will homeschooling cure awkwardness unless you purposefully teach social skills and provide a lot of social interaction instruction to overcome awkwardness.

I know that is a bit of an aside from the topic of learning styles, but it seemed a good place to address the concerns people sometimes have about meeting a child's individual needs, sociability, and concerns about how much individualization is "too much." As long as you address your child's needs in a functional way without leading him to believe the entire world revolves around his every need, you and your child should be okay. Having a child whose needs are met is infinitely better than having a child whose needs are neglected because of a societal judgment about "catering to the child."

Unstructured Learning

We can't consider education outside of the box without looking at the form of homeschooling known as "unschooling." Unschooling is learning without doing "school" per se. Unschoolers seek to learn naturally throughout their days, and typical activities for the child's learning are intrinsically self-driven. The child decides what he wants to learn, when he wants to learn it, and the method by which he will learn it.

The unschooling model follows after typical learning you would see in the early development of any child. Consider an infant who learns to sit, then stand, then walk; who learns the names of foods, objects, people, etc. The child is never explicitly taught the early concepts. He learns them through exposure, through hearing the names of items and associating them with the object, and through practice. Unschooling carries this form of natural learning forward in the natural progression of life with the thought that if a child needs or wants to know algebra, he can teach himself when he is ready and open to learning the topic.

Hardcore unschoolers also tend take a very hands-off approach to any type of learning issues or disabilities. They believe that a child will teach himself to read when he is ready to learn to read. If you are attracted to the idea of unschooling, be aware that your child may never choose to learn to read or do algebra. If that is fine with you and fine with your child, then unschooling might be viable for you.

Consider also that unschooling may be attractive to a parent because she doesn't have to make lesson plans, grade her child's assignments, or otherwise drive her child's education. However, if a child wants to go into a field that requires a college degree, a young child doesn't really understand what is required for college. For example, reading is required for college, but if the child finds reading difficult, he may not press himself to learn to read or to delve into other required subjects. We know a couple of young men who feel their moms failed to meet their educational needs because the moms did not prepare them adequately for college. The young men could—at any time—decide to do whatever needs to be done in order to get into college. Thus, it isn't really the mom's "fault" these days, but a child's failure to learn all that is needed while being homeschooled can be a significant issue for any young adult.

When considering what form to have your homeschooling take, 100 percent unschooling takes a level of faith in a child's self-driven need to learn, which I often think has been driven out of a child if he has spent much time in a traditional school. Some children aren't all that driven "to know," and their curiosity level is low enough that they'd rather spend all of their time playing than pursuing any level of academia. Differences in personality alone can make a child one which I would consider a perfect unschooler versus a child who will learn nothing if unschooled.

As an example of how unschooling works, let me share with you one of my son's learning explorations. One day my son was watching the StarGate TV show and he wondered about the Egyptian God, Ra. He began to research Ra and encountered information about Greek mythology, so he began to study the Greek gods and Greek culture. He realized then that some of the Greek mythology characters were also the names of some of the constellations he had heard of, so he began studying astronomy. As he studied astronomy, he became interested in the planets and stars and what they were made of, which led him to delve into chemistry. Before I knew it, he was cataloging (looking up and writing down) the chemical make-up of all common forms of rock.

My older son is so motivated just to KNOW that he is very self-driven in his learning. My son studied all of these subjects under his own initiative outside of the traditional academic work I had assigned to him. This is how unschooling is supposed to work. We were not unschoolers, but I always thought my older son was the perfect example of a self-driven learner ideal for unschooling.

Given my older son's propensity toward self-driven learning, one year I thought we'd give unschooling a try. My younger son was not a self-driven learner when he was young. He would prefer to play all day, every day, and he just wasn't that curious about the world around him. He was perfectly happy knowing what he knew and staying in the realm of his own knowledge. It became fairly obvious that my younger son wasn't going to learn much at all unless he had traditional schoolwork placed in front of him. Thus, we always felt a need to undertake some degree of traditional schooling in addition to letting our boys explore areas of interest.

If unschooling seems appealing to you and you aren't concerned about any educational gaps your child may develop, I'd suggest carefully weighing your child's level of curiosity and natural inclination toward learning-based explorations. While some homeschoolers are 100 percent unschoolers, most homeschooling families I know study traditional academics for some portion of their day. Depending upon how self-driven to learn your child(ren) may be, you can gauge how much pre-planned study to undertake using more traditional teaching and learning methods.

At a minimum, I would suggest ensuring your child knows how to read, how to write, and how to perform math calculations. If any one of these areas is gravely difficult for your child and/or he has a learning disability in the area, I would suggest undertaking robust educational programs to teach these core concept skills. The big three of reading, writing, and performing math calculations are required to function in almost any job or profession a person might undertake as an adult. Making sure your child has mastered the basic functional skills needed by any adult will at least ensure a minimal level of preparedness for lifelong career pursuits.

Given that most everyone I know who homeschools undertakes a mix of traditional academics and unschooling, I would suggest filling your mornings with traditional, core academics and allowing your afternoons to be open for pursuing passions, clubs, activities, sports, etc. Leaving the evenings or weekends open for fun, family, and friends helps fill the days of the week in a well-rounded schedule.

Just remember that homeschooling allows you to be flexible about your scheduling, academics, passionate pursuits, and social calendar. While the previous example is based upon the type of scheduling most of the families we know use, including ourselves, your schedule should fit the rhythms and needs of your family.

Homeschooling can be as rigid or flexible as you want to make it. Most families, parents and children alike, enjoy having a mix of structured study time and time for self-determined activities. You can school any way you like as long as you meet legal homeschooling requirements in your state.

Feeding Passions

On the heels of unschooling, which is 100 percent passion driven, let's talk about the pursuit of passionate interests. Whatever your child's interest, help him pursue it with passion. Homeschooling provides a unique opportunity for you to let your child explore avenues of interest with greater depth and breadth than he would be able to undertake if his life was driven by the demands of traditional schooling.

When your child is in public or private school, he is classroom taught and at the mercy of the teacher's assignment scheduling, required homework, and time in school. If he has outside activities as well, your child will not have a lot of free time to hone a skill, grow in a talent, or pursue a new passion of interest.

Consider child actors. They are virtually all taught one-on-one by a tutor. Yes, they are working children, but most of them are pursuing a passion for acting. Similarly, young athletes, dancers, musicians, etc., often pursue their interests in specialized learning environments that provide their education in a scheduled format that optimizes the child's ability to pursue his or her passion. Homeschooling easily provides the opportunity for your child to similarly pursue a passionate interest without the limitations driven by traditional schooling.

If your child struggles with academics, completing all of the homework assigned in a traditional school can leave the child with no time to pursue passions. Having no areas of interest to pursue, nor time to do anything other than complete schoolwork, can drain any person's spirit.

As previously mentioned, my older son took a long time to complete schoolwork because of his struggles with dyslexia. He couldn't complete his classroom work in the allotted time, so the teacher would "let" him bring the uncompleted work home. His entire evenings were full of more schoolwork, homework, exhaustion, and nothing fun whatsoever. Traditional schooling was draining his spirit and his time.

Enter homeschooling. Because I could read my son's books aloud and he could dictate his answers to me, the amount of time he spent on academic learning was shortened. We worked on reading skills diligently for two hours per day for three years until he could read proficiently by himself. After two hours of reading instruction, I would read his science and social studies books to him and allow him to orally answer the questions. That saved a boatload of time and actually allowed us to complete our traditional academics around 2:00 in the afternoon. Then what?

My son really had no outside interests during the school year because he had never had time for anything while he was going to public school. His life was school, homework, and sleep and school, homework, and sleep. One day I was reading our local homeschool newsletter and saw there was a kayak program for homeschoolers. I asked my son casually if he'd like to try kayaking. He said, "YES!" I was a bit surprised because I had no idea he'd like to try boating of any kind. I signed him up for the next instructional session for kayaking, and the rest was history.

Kayaking became a passion for my son and still is. He learned sprint kayaking, raced in races, won medals, saved his money, bought his own kayak, and still kayaks recreationally with friends whenever he gets a chance.

Had we not been homeschooling, my son never would have had the opportunity to try kayaking given his full day of demands from the public school and homework. In addition to exploring kayaking, my son tried fencing, tennis, archery (still a love of his also), guitar, basketball, and other opportunities.

Our younger son pursued a wide variety of passions— more than his older brother. It was more difficult for my younger son to find something that he loved to do over and over and over again. Our younger son tried soccer, ice skating, fencing, basketball, tennis, archery, golf, game programming, piano, guitar, drums, bowling, kayaking, rowing, and probably a few other interests I've missed.

Having the opportunity to explore various passions of the moment and finding a couple of pursuits that will be lifelong interests helped my younger son find his place in the world. Without these homeschooling activity opportunities, my son could not have ruled out such a wide variety of options and found activities of interest to him.

If your child is oppressed by the traditional school setting he or she is in, and if you are able to homeschool, you could very well open up a world of unimaginable possibilities to your child through homeschooling and the pursuit of passions. I never dreamed when we began homeschooling that I would end up with an archery-loving kayaker who is a passionate scientist, and a music-loving drummer who is a competitive bowler, but that is what we ended up with.

If your child is labeled a "trouble maker" in school because he is bored, an active learner, or otherwise wants to pursue passions outside of pure academics, homeschooling could be an answered prayer for your child too. For children who are bright but bored with traditional school, the tedious time in the classroom can be endless torture. My younger son began expressing his annoyance with the tediousness of the traditional classroom when he was in first grade. FIRST GRADE! My younger son can learn most things with one period of instruction, but typical public school teachers go over the same concept repeatedly so that the entire class can grasp the concept. For a child who understands the concept the first time around, the additional repetition is tedious.

Apply the tediousness, boredom, slower-than-snails learning pace to a gifted child with attention deficit hyperactivity disorder and you have a recipe for class-clowning, discipline problems, or both. The long school days are draining and boring, and so much of the child's potential is wasted. Students who stay bored in school are wasting the level of academic achievement or talent potential he or she might achieve if given the freedom to pursue education and passions at their own pace.

Consider my younger son. He is smart as a whip and can crank out answers to math calculations faster than you can line your numbers up in a column. In the second grade, his teacher drilled him over and over and over to see just how fast he could work 100 math problems. It was an amazing speed game for the teacher, but it was tedious, pointless drilling to my son. While the teacher was entertained, my son was growing more disenchanted with public school each day and began begging me to homeschool him. What second grader even knows what homeschooling is? Mine did, and he wanted it!

My husband and I were slower on the uptake. When our son's teacher told us she didn't want to advance the math instruction for our young son because he'd be "even more bored next school year," it was obvious the public school environment was holding our son back academically. I mentioned in the introduction that my son's boredom and ADHD began to surface as clowning around, which included a couple of visits to the principal's office for his mischief. We began to see where feeding our son's passion for math would serve him well and he would be better served at home. So we took our second-grader's advice and began homeschooling.

At the time, we believed we began homeschooling because our younger son wanted to and our older son needed to homeschool, but the truth is that both sons needed it. Watching friends' and neighbors' children who were similarly bored in school grow into young adults has shown their outcomes to be difficult and sometimes undesirable. From skipping school, dropping out of school, to drug use, under-achievement, and even being criminalized by the school for acting out, it is clear to me that unmet educational needs can lead to any number of undesirable outcomes. As parents, we have the need and responsibility to ensure that our children's educational needs are met even if that means meeting them ourselves through homeschooling.

If you see any unmet educational need in your child's life, whether directly or indirectly related to traditional schooling, think about homeschooling and its possibilities. Whether your child's passion is academics, a special talent, or you need to provide an opportunity for your child to find a passion, homeschooling can help your child pursue a path that propels him forward.

Truthfully, I had no clue how well homeschooling would

meet our sons' psychological, learning, emotional, and esteem needs when we first decided to homeschool. However, being able to pursue academics and interests with a passion has been among the greatest benefits of homeschooling for our boys. No matter what issue or problem is holding your child back, if you homeschool, you can arrange your days academically and in the pursuit of interests in whatever way best meets your child's needs. Being able to feed your child's passions and academic interests can lead to better achievement and unexpectedly amazing outcomes.

SANDRA K. COOK

6 ECONOMIC SURVIVAL

By nature, the vast majority of homeschooling families have only one income. As difficult as it may be financially, we all made the choice to homeschool because it is what is best for our children and our children are our highest priority—they are above bigger houses, new cars, exciting vacations, etc. If you are a single-income family that survives well on one income, be thankful you can homeschool without hardship.

There are homeschooling families in which both parents work, but those cases are few and far between. It is possible to work and homeschool, but it is difficult. If you happen to be one of those families where working is a requirement, it can be done, but you will need extra support and assistance. There is a "Work and Homeschool" Yahoo! Group that provides support, creative ideas for managing challenging situations, and daily management ideas for working parents who are also trying to homeschool. You can join the group at http://groups.yahoo.com/group/WORKandHOMESCHOOL/.

For those of us who are able to survive on one income, the economic road can be challenging. There are some homeschooling families whose income level is high enough that homeschooling does not create any hardship, but the majority of homeschooling families have to make adjustments to their priorities, be frugal, and reduce expenditures wherever possible. In this chapter we examine steps you can take to survive economically while homeschooling.

Cutting Back

Most homeschooling moms I know had careers prior to becoming homeschoolers. The majority of us gave up a job to stay home with our children and have therefore suffered a decline in income at the same time that we incurred the additional cost of educating our children. Having previously had ample income, there are many activities or goods a family might be accustomed to having which will need to be re-examined as expenses to determine if the cash outlay is affordable on an ongoing basis.

Let's look at some adjustments homeschoolers tend to make to reduce expenses. Thinking about adjustments you may have to make will help you decide if homeschooling on one income is a lifestyle change you can live with for the duration of your homeschooling. These are areas where I know homeschooling families tend to make cuts, so I think they are the most realistic in terms of lifestyle adjustments for the sake of homeschooling.

When a family is a two-income family with children in school, the demands of work and school often mean that time to cook and prepare meals gives way to dining out. If you begin homeschooling, your schedule will likely be less hectic, giving you more time to cook, plus your income will be less and that will make it more difficult to dine out. There is a trade-off that can be made: Cooking at home can be a wonderful math activity (measuring & portioning), provide reading practice (recipes), and help your child develop a needed life-skill if you engage in cooking with your children.

As homeschoolers who cook at home most of the time, we have planned out our menus for the year. Once each summer I sit down and plan out our menus for the entire year so that management of family dinners is clearly laid out, making it easy for everyone to participate in meal preparation. It also helps us to know what coupons we'll need so that we can begin collecting those ahead of time. We are not an extreme-couponing family, but I know a couple of homeschooling families who participate in extreme couponing, which saves them a lot of money on groceries.

After you begin homeschooling, you will be with your children most of the time. While texting and talking on the phone are prevalent activities among teens, these activities are not a necessity. Premium cell phone plans are expensive, so we adopted a "phones for emergencies" mindset. We use our cell phones only when we need to during those times when one of our children is participating in a class or function without a parent nearby. Truthfully, we found we didn't need expensive plans at all and went with a basic cell phone plan for one phone and a "go phone" for the other. When we left a child at an activity, the child would have possession of one cell phone and a parent would have the other cell phone. Operating this way minimized the amount of money we paid each month for cell phones.

One of the best things about being among homeschoolers are the discounts which are made available to the community, including teacher discounts at bookstores, office supply places, admissions to museums, etc. By participating in activities via homeschool channels, you can broaden your child's exposure to a wider variety of opportunities without paying full cost. While you are spending less money than you would have spent at full price, you are nevertheless spending money. Thus, participating with homeschool groups in activities and on field trips, buying things at a discount, etc. can still be expensive. Your income may limit the number of opportunities you are able to participate in, but it is always good to know there are discounts available to help lessen the amount of money you might have spent otherwise.

Cutting out cable or cable channels both saves money and helps with school compliance. Many homeschool families opt for Netflix and online viewing of shows. Families like Netflix in particular because they have a good selection of documentaries that you can use in your homeschooling. Additionally, the programs are commercial free. Personally, we checked out countless educational DVDs from our local library rather than use Netflix. Cutting cable isn't a favorable cost-cutting option for some families, but it is an option if you need to cut costs. Of course, you don't have to have any such programming if you don't want to. Some families opt for no TV at all.

A great way to save money is for your family to do as much of the household work as possible. Tasks such as cleaning, car washing, lawn care, haircuts—anything service oriented—can be accomplished at home as a joint family effort. We always say our home is not a country club, but a working co-op. As an example, consider situations where your carpet may need shampooing. We found it was cheaper to buy a household carpet shampooer than to pay a major carpet-cleaning company to come and clean the carpets for us. Our shampooer has paid for itself repeatedly as we have used it on numerous spills, stains, and to remove water when a leak left our carpet soggy.

A couple of other cost-cutting measures are reducing gift-giving levels and giving educational items (art supplies, musical instruments, science kits, etc.) as gifts to the children while having the children make homemade gifts for each other and the parents. I'm currently in possession of a "Car Wash Coupon Book" with coupons that entitle me to "on demand" car washes from my son. I LOVE having the book at my disposal, and it is a great way for my sons to find creative ways to give gifts and serve others.

While many of our double-income friends drive new cars, driving old cars and carpooling with homeschool friends saves us a lot of money. Given that a car loses the majority of its value when it is driven off the lot, it makes sense to buy low-mileage used cars from a reliable source, and then drive the cars until they become more costly to own than obtaining another car might be. Because gas costs are high, homeschoolers carpool to distant events as much as logistics allow. Carpooling is particularly helpful for cutting costs when the destination is a state or national park, where admission is on a per vehicle basis or where there is a parking fee.

As an example, Six Flags offers an annual "Homeschool Day" in the spring of each school year. Although everyone must pay for individual (discounted) admission to the park regardless of the number of people in the vehicle, having only one vehicle means there is less money expended in parking fees. Additionally, because there is a payment-processing charge, usually homeschoolers will collectively order and divide the processing charge among the families buying tickets. For an individual family, if we reduce the charge to $2, $3, or even $4 per family, it is a nice savings off the current $12 charge for ordering tickets online and having them sent in the mail.

A more unusual cost-saving measure that I've known a couple families to take advantage of is to move to a smaller house. Personally, we have chosen to stay in our home as we have watched all of the "upwardly mobile" families around us buy bigger, fancier homes and move away. We are only one of a couple families on our street who have remained here through the years of raising our boys. Staying in the same home has given our boys a strong sense of stability and strong ties to their hometown. By staying in this home, our mortgage balance is low and our payments are comparatively low, which made it easier for us to weather the economic downturn. Although our home is older, there are many cost-saving benefits of remaining here for the long-term.

Although it is not a cost-saving measure, hiring a homeschool worker to complete any jobs for which skilled labor is needed helps other homeschooling families. Whether you need trees taken down, plumbing help, HVAC work, etc., by hiring a homeschooling parent, you are likely to get a homeschool community discount and/or help another homeschooling family continue to homeschool. Some of the best work we have had done has been provided by companies run by homeschooling dads.

You may have been able to think of many of these cost-saving ideas yourself, and there are other ways people save money, but I thought you might find a measure of comfort regarding finances to know that other homeschooling families have cut costs in similar ways. The homeschool community is wonderful about helping and supporting each other.

As online charter schools pull in more would-be homeschooling families though, there is a slight trend toward weakening the homeschool community bonds. In other words, it may be a bit more difficult to find other true homeschooling families as the years progress. It's worth noting too: Those who use online charter schools are becoming a community unto themselves, so it may—in reality—be a shift in the community rather than a weakening of the community.

Supplemental Income from Home

Almost every homeschooling family I know has, at times, needed an extra boost of income to help support the desires of the family. I hesitate to say "to support the needs of the family" because usually the need for extra income is to pay for an expensive interest of a child, such as fencing, horseback riding, learning to fly, or some other activity that requires a higher outlay of cash than the family can easily afford. Thus, the family can feed itself, clothe itself, and have a roof over their heads without a problem, but a family may need to find creative ways to pay for activities, interests, or educational opportunities they would like to provide for their child(ren).

As a mom, you can have fun and earn extra income in many different ways. The most common way moms earn extra income is to teach other people's children a skill or academic subject. You can form "classes" and offer them to the homeschool community in your area of passion, skill, or interest, and if you are near any sizable homeschooling community, you will likely have enough children who are interested to form a class. We know moms who teach sewing, painting, creative writing, chemistry, biology, high school math, drama, any kind of musical instrument (piano, guitar, band), etc. Many moms will offer to teach individual lessons or group classes for $20-$50 per month. If you are knowledgeable about any of the high school subjects, you are very likely to be able to offer and fill a class.

For example, many moms neither want to nor have the background to teach biology and dissection. The homeschooling mom that I know who loves biology and dissection is able to fill a class with a good number of students. Given she has 10 students who each pay her $45 per month for the class, she is earning an extra $450 per month to help make ends meet.

Another parent teaches each of the high school-level math courses for about $60 per month, per student. Given he teaches Algebra 1, Algebra 2, geometry, pre-calculus and calculus, each with a dozen students in the class (he fills his classes and is in demand), he earns about $3,600 per month teaching math two days per week. The students come for a question-and-answer day and a lab day. The students are taught new content, given their assignments for the week (which they turn in the following week, are graded and returned the next week), and the teacher tracks all grades and progress. For moms who don't know high school mathematics, having someone to teach the courses is of great help.

At-home marketing programs like Premier jewelry, Mary Kay make-up, It Works!, Pampered Chef, etc. are also popular among homeschooling moms. The marketing programs allow the moms to homeschool during the day, to coordinate their business efforts when it is convenient for them, and hostess purchasing parties in the evenings.

Some moms use their talents for product creation and sales—jewelry, mounted photographs, painting, T-shirt printing, etc.—which they sell via avenues like Etsy.com, eBay, or at local venues. The moms work on making items in the evening and on weekends, packaging and shipping as orders come in.

Other moms and I offer support to the homeschool community throughout the United States and the world through online website or product offerings. Several homeschooling moms have created products they sell online to the homeschooling community, such as:

- Phyllis Wheeler's "Nurturing Your Asperger's Child,"
- Lee Binz's Total Transcript Solution program, or
- Terri Johnson's 26-week Homeschooling ABCs class.

My website, LearningAbledKids.com, has provided a small income through the Google AdSense and Amazon.com's affiliate programs. Traditionally, I've not had a product to sell of my own, and my affiliate income will never make me rich, but it has provided a nice buffer to make it the activities, outings, and supplies we've needed affordable. The small income has provided a wide variety of educational opportunities for our boys.

With a bit of creative thinking as to how to market your strengths, you may be able to supplement your family's income while homeschooling your child. To survive, a family usually requires one stably employed adult to provide for the basic needs of the family, but you would be surprised how little a family can survive on when they are willing to sacrifice material things in exchange for excellence in education at home.

Cost-Effective Homeschooling

Aside from household survival, there is an added cost to homeschooling a child because you must buy educational supplies. However, there are members of the homeschool community who homeschool their children for free, using free resources, and many who homeschool with minimal expenditure. If you are willing to research and find most of the content and coursework your child needs, there are numerous free resources available through the Internet and libraries that will enable you to homeschool for little or no money, educationally speaking. Let's look at some of the ways people cut costs in their home education provisioning.

Knowing What to Teach with Inexpensive Resources

One of the first aspects of home education that usually concerns new families is what to teach and when to teach it. While there are books such as What your ?th Grader Needs to Know, similar information can easily be obtained for free by looking at various state standards for learning on state Department of Education websites. To find standards for learning, simply go to any major search engine and type in "learning standards" and add your state's name if you'd like standards specific to your state. However, you do not have to have standards specific to your state unless you are legally required to follow those standards. Any standards for learning will serve as a checklist for figuring out what your child would be learning at any grade level if he or she were in the public school system.

While you may be concerned about following standards, think back to your own primary and secondary schooling. For all of the facts, figures, dates, and details you were taught, what percentage of that information can you quickly and easily recall today? If you are like most people, you can recall only a small fraction of the information you were required to memorize and regurgitate for tests while you were in school. Aside from knowing how to read, how to use math for daily life, and knowing how to communicate in written form, most of the academic body of knowledge can be researched at any point in time when a specific fact may need to be known. Therefore, it really isn't necessary to obsess about whether your child knows or learns every detail outlined in the state standards for learning.

If your child acquires a good understanding of the broader concept, then he is likely to be adequately educated to survive in life. This doesn't mean you'd want to be slack about educating your child by any means, but do not stress about memorization and testing to the same degree the public schools do. They are focused on high testing outcomes because their funding depends upon it, but fact memorization and testing is not necessary for the overall educational advancement of a child's understanding of the world around him.

Aside from using state standards to determine what to teach your child, there are several online sources with free or inexpensive homeschool plans, books, and other resources. The most popular site I know of that offers free homeschooling curricula is AmblesideOnline.org. According to their website: "Ambleside Online uses the highest quality books and costs no more than the cost of texts. The curriculum uses as many free online books as possible, and there is no cost to use this information or join the support group." MANY families I know use Ambleside Online for their primary educational plans.

A website that is becoming more widely used is KhanAcademy.org whose tag line is "Learn almost anything for free." Khan is an excellent resource for teaching using video and audio, which are ideal for children who require audio-visual input to improve their learning. While Khan is not laid out with curricula plans, you can have your child select any topic and progress through all related lessons. In our homeschool, we have used Khan as a resource alongside inexpensive books for teaching and learning.

For example, you can buy an older algebra book with a solutions manual very inexpensively through eBay, Half.com, or Amazon.com. Although it is just an algebra book, your child can read the chapters and access videos at Khan Academy or PurpleMath.com to gain a full understanding of the concepts being taught. Your child can then work the problems, and you can check them against the solutions manual.

You can also purchase discounted curricula or learning programs through providers that seek to provide cost-effective solutions. One popular discount provider is the HomeschoolBuyersCo-Op.org. This Co-op seeks discount pricing as a large purchaser on behalf of the collective of homeschooling families. The Co-op purchases programs in bulk lots at a discount or makes arrangements for discount purchasing through providers, and then offers the discount pricing to homeschool families who wish to purchase the products. We have purchased several programs through the Co-op and were very pleased with the pricing and the products.

Providers of curricula and learning products to the homeschool market often hold sales sometime between May and September of each year. If you decide you'd like to use a particular program, product, or books, sign up for newsletter mailings and watch for sales announcements. Most providers I know offer a sale sometime at the end or the beginning of each school year.

There are also used curriculum sales among various groups in the homeschool community. If you have an idea what types of books or curricula you need or want for your child, you can go to the used curriculum sales, usually held at the end of each school year, and buy used curricula from other homeschooling families at a great discount. Seldom did we buy anything new. When you go to the curriculum sales, the prices are usually less than half of the retail cost, and you can look at the items before you buy them.

Participating in the used curriculum sales is a great way to sell your used books and purchase your next years' books without much, if any, additional outlay of cash. In the beginning, of course you will have to spend more to acquire your first year or two of teaching materials, and you won't always sell everything you've put up for sale, but over time your sales will come close to your needed purchases at the used curricula sales. When you approach the end of your homeschooling days, you can sell your books at a used curriculum sale and keep the cash.

An additional need for homeschooling is supplies. While schools spend a great deal for flashcards, manipulatives, etc., you can make your own flashcards using blank index cards or purchase sets cheaply at the used curriculum sales. Office Depot, Office Max, Staples, and other suppliers give discounts to teachers and will give you the teacher discount based upon your homeschooling documentation. Similarly, if you need any software products, most software companies offer discounted academic versions of their software, so be certain to research and see if there is an academic version available to you for a deep discount. Microsoft and Adobe are two companies that offer deep discounts to teachers.

When you are considering which programs you'd like to use and what materials you'll need, be sure to search for discounted products, sales, and used curricula purchase opportunities in addition to free resources. You can save your family quite a bit of money for your actual schooling endeavor by using these suggestions and coming up with creative avenues for buying, selling, and trading materials you need for teaching.

Free or Inexpensive Teaching Resources

As mentioned in the previous section, you can use free teaching resources online such as KhanAcademy.org, PurpleMath.com, or AmblesideOnline.org. In addition to these great resources, truthfully you can find just about anything you want or need for teaching your child somewhere online.

These days, there are countless educational videos available for viewing on YouTube. When my sons encountered a difficult topic that didn't make sense when reading about it, I searched on YouTube to find two or three quality videos that explain the concept. You do have to wade through a number of poor-quality or inadequate videos in order to find what you need, but if you desire to home educate for low or no cost, you can use this resource to otherwise eliminate the need to hire a teacher to teach your child. The key is having open communications and frequent discussions with your student to know when you need to find supplementary teaching materials.

Sites like NASA, the National Institute of Health, the History Channel, Discovery Channel, and National Geographic all have great educational content. Some attractions, like Sea World and Zoo Atlanta, have high quality educational sections within their websites where your child can learn about animals, plants, or other topics of interest. For any given area of study your child may undertake, you are likely to be able to find a high-quality web resource for your child to explore.

If you are using the state standards for learning as a guideline to teaching your child, you can check out topic-related books from the library and seek out online websites with quality information. Using these three tools, you can provide your child a high-quality, comprehensive education at little or no expense to you.

As your child grows up and enters high school, you can use open university initiatives as mentioned previously and textbook publishers' resource sections to find targeted content for academic studies. You will recall that Massachusetts Institute of Technology (MIT) has an open course initiative you can find at: http://ocw.mit.edu/index.htm. Through the MIT Open Course initiative, you can access lecture videos, syllabi, and exams, providing complete courses in a large number of topics. Generally speaking, each course utilizes a particular textbook, which you would have to purchase, but all other content is free.

Taking courses through the MIT Open Course initiative does NOT provide college credit of any kind, but provides you with a comprehensive course for advanced subjects your child needs to study for high school. Other similar initiatives to the MIT Open Course initiative can be found at:

- ITunes Open University
- Open University
- Open Yale
- Harvard Open Learning Initiative
- Stanford University's Open Classroom

I'm certain there are many resources available that I have yet to discover, but you can uncover them by searching online based upon the topic(s) your child is studying.

In addition to the open courseware, you will find many unit studies, worksheets, and teacher resources available for free online. The US government has a free teachers' resource section found at: http://free.ed.gov/. Two other sites frequently used by homeschooling parents are Teacher Created Resources http://www.teachercreated.com/free/ and the Scholastic Books Teachers' Site, http://teacher.scholastic.com/resources-for-teachers/. You can also find great, free unit studies at: http://homehearts.com/category/units/.

With a little bit of creativity, planning, and searching, you can find resources that will enable you to homeschool your child for free. While we did not homeschool our boys for free, we reduced costs significantly by using a wide variety of resources that were available to us. We have friends who homeschooled for very little money, and others who desired to purchase everything new and did so.

We also know families in which the parents were overwhelmed at the thought of teaching, planning, and acquiring all of the needed resources, so they purchased comprehensive solutions from online providers. The Alpha Omega Monarch Academy, Bob Jones University Press's Online High School, and Liberty University's Online High School are three commonly used options.

For many of our high school courses, we used Marshall University's Online College Classes for High School. Marshall's courses are inexpensive, and they count for both high school and college credit. Taking the Marshall University courses, CLEP exams (similar to AP exams used by traditional schools), and local dual-enrollment courses allowed each of my sons to begin attending their chosen universities as sophomores, having completed several credit hours past the completion of their freshman year while still in high school. See: http://clep.collegeboard.org/exam for more information about CLEP exams, and be aware that not all colleges grant credit for CLEP exams.

As you can see, no matter what your family income level is, there are materials available that will enable you to homeschool your child. You can pursue completely free resources or pay to have all of the teaching, materials, scheduling, and oversight provided to your child. The avenue you pursue is limited only by your own personal values and finances, which may or may not match completely. However, homeschooling your child is viable given adequate financial provisioning to meet the daily living needs of your family. Educationally, the materials can be acquired for free, but it will require additional creativity, research, and planning on your part.

7 CONCLUSION

More Than You Can Imagine

As I hope you realize by now, there is much more to the homeschooling world and lifestyle than most people imagine. Before entering into the homeschooling community, people generally know very little about the day-to-day hows, whos, and whys of home educating their child. I know my personal knowledge regarding what it was like to homeschool was only a fraction of the total lifestyle package. I had a number of misconceptions and areas of complete ignorance.

Through this book, I hope I have opened your eyes and filled your mind with different ways of thinking about and understanding the homeschooling world. From educational opportunities to social benefits, from lifestyle enhancements to financial difficulties, you now have a much better understanding of what homeschooling will be like for you, your spouse, and your children than most people do before they dive into this world. It is really an amazing, often fun, and sometimes challenging way of educating your children.

Can't Start Soon Enough

With all I've said, I hope you're as excited about getting started homeschooling as I have been about sharing this insider information with you. Before we began homeschooling, I was very apprehensive and my hesitation was mired in concerns about my own inadequacies, stereotypes of homeschoolers, and questions about how it would affect my children. In hindsight, the only thing I would have done differently in the beginning would be to start homeschooling sooner!

My only regret has been wasting the time we spent waffling, trying to decide about homeschooling, trying to pursue other educational solutions for our sons, when in reality, diving into homeschooling at the soonest hint of trouble with pubic school would have saved us a couple of years of heartache.

So, I hope your local homeschooling community will welcome you with open arms. Start your online searches today to find homeschoolers near you, connect with them, and learn about the various homeschooling activities and opportunities near you. You won't believe the fantastical journey that awaits your family if you choose to travel the homeschooling path.

If you've decided to venture forth with homeschooling, and your child has dyslexia, you may want to check out Sandy's latest book, *How To Defeat Your Child's Dyslexia*. Whether you're just starting homeschooling or are just realizing your child has learning problems, this book can help you learn how to meet the unique challenges of home schooling your Learning Abled Kid.

Now that you've finished this book, I hope you have found it to be helpful and informative. If you could take a minute to leave a review and rate this book on Amazon, your review will help other parents of Learning Abled Kids know if this book will help them make a decision about whether to homeschool their learning abled kid. Of course, I hope you've gained a lot of information and insight which will encourage you that you can meet the educational needs of your child through homeschooling.

HAPPY HOMESCHOOLING!

REFERENCES

Delquadri, J., Duval, S., & Ward,D., (2004). A preliminary investigation of the effectiveness of homeschool instructional environments for students with attention-deficit/hyperactivity disorder. School Psychology Review, Volume 33, Number 1, 140-158. Copyright 2004 by the National Association of School Psychologists, Bethesda, MD. Reprinted with permission of the publisher. www.nasponline.org.

Ensign, J., (2000). Defying the stereotypes of special education: Home school students. Peabody Journal of Education. Volume 75, Number 1 & 2, 147-158.

For additional information or support, visit:
http://LearningAbledKids.com/
https://www.facebook.com/LearningAbledKids
https://twitter.com/LearnAbledKids

If you have a child with special learning needs, join our support Group for homeschooling children with learning differences:
https://groups.yahoo.com/neo/groups/LearningAbledKids.

SANDRA K. COOK

ABOUT THE AUTHOR

Sandra K. Cook is a veteran homeschooling mom. While homeschooling, Sandra, a.k.a. Sandy, earned her Master's Degree in Instructional Design and Technology and graduated Summa Cum Laude. Sandy completed Orton-Gillingham Multisensory training (for teaching reading to children with dyslexia), Georgia Advocacy Office's Parent Leadership Support Project Advocacy training, Georgia Charter School Association's "Organization and Concept Development" Training, is a Petitioner for American Sign Language for Georgia Students, is a Lifetime Member of Phi Kappa Phi Academic Honor Society, and an educational change advocate.

Sandy provides resources, information, and support for parents homeschooling children with learning disabilities through the company she founded, Learning Abled Kids, L.L.C.. She operates an online support group hosted on the Yahoo! Groups platform, which has well over 1500 members, and provides information and resources through her website: (http://LearningAbledKids.com).

Sandy is also the author of *How To Defeat Your Child's Dyslexia* and *Cook's Prize Winning Annual Meal Planning System: "Plan once per year and you are done!"* Both books are available on Amazon.com.

Recreationally, Sandy enjoys spending time with her family, photography, bowling, kayaking, writing, and walking with God.

CPSIA information can be obtained
at www.ICGtesting.com
Printed in the USA
LVOW04s1532120416
483256LV00014B/791/P

9 781490 921228